THE WAY THINGS WERE SERIES

MAIN

An Anthology edited by Donna Talarico

Books by Hippocampus
A Division of Hippocampus Magazine, LLC

THE WAY THINGS WERE SERIES

MAIN

An Anthology edited by Donna Talarico

"Last Stand in the Closing Country" first appeared in *Brevity* in January 2007

"Reflections on My Grandmother's Costume Shop While Anxiously Making Masks" first appeared in *Hippocampus Magazine* in January/February 2021

"What Needs Done: The Love and Burden of a Family Business" first appeared at *LitHub* in April 2021

Published by:
Books by Hippocampus
An imprint of Hippocampus Magazine and Books LLC
210 W. Grant Street, Suite 104
Lancaster, PA 17603

books.hippocampusmagazine.com | books@hippocampusmagazine.com

ISBN: 9780999429945
First printing, November 2021

Cover design: Lindsay Enochs
Book layout by: Stefany A. Salazar R.

Printed in the United States of America

TABLE OF CONTENTS

INTRODUCTION

I grew up in the Poconos, a rural, mountainous area where you weren't likely to find sidewalks, at least where I spent time. So when I visited my aunt, uncle, and cousins in the tiny town of Hartshorne, Oklahoma, in the early 1990s, I fell in love with the block-or-so-long main street strip. (My cousins actually lived in neighboring Haileyville—the other "Twin City"—home to a quirky general store with shampoo and conditioner bottles that sat on the shelves so long, the contents had started to separate.)

My mom and I ended up settling about an hour north in Tulsa, a major city with conveniences I'd never experienced, like a Taco Bell right on my block. Still, I longed for the feeling I got on that small strip of storefronts in Hartshorne, which, at the time, was mostly empty, save for a pool hall (called "The Rec") and one or two businesses I cannot recall. Still, shuttered or not, this tight-knit cluster introduced me to the idea of Main Street.

Today, whenever I go on road trips, I love exploring small-town main street districts. Often, they are ghost towns, remnants of once-booming business districts. Sometimes, they're still bustling, a mix of long-time businesses hanging on with a few new mom-and-pop additions to the street. Other times, they appear to still have that small-town charm, but on second glance, you realize they are clearly glitzed up, gentrified versions of their past selves. Experiencing the varying conditions and activity of Main Street USA inspired *Main*.

♦

I struggle to eloquently define "main street." For me, aside from the physicality of a block or two of neat, old architecture, "main street" is simply a feeling I get. Luckily, I found a solid description of the "classic main street." In their 2018 *Journal of Urban Design* article, "Does the Classic American Main Street Still Exist? An Exploratory Look," Emily Talen and Hyesun Jeng list eight key characteristics: mixed use, sidewalks, more small businesses than chains, at least one daily service (like a grocery store), at least one amenity (such as a bar or cafe), at least one older (pre-1950) building, no major degrading visual factor (like a big parking lot), and a real sense of enclosure (which is described as "building-height-to-street-width ratio.")

In a 2018 *Medium* interview with Talen about her study of Chicago-area main streets, she explains areas like these have universal charm because, "It's part of the public realm. It's not the kind of public space you just go to recreate or hang out. This is a public space that's kind of part of your daily routine."

When you think about the main streets you've experienced—then and now—do they (or did they) fit this description? Could they again?

♦

The automobile. The suburbs. Malls. Big box stores. Ecommerce. All of these have contributed to the decline of countless main streets across the United States. In many places, though, there's a resurgence of these districts, oftentimes resulting in a more inclusive and richer selection of independent businesses. (In my city of Lancaster, Pennsylvania, for instance, an amazing organization called Assets is helping empower entrepreneurs–and has a strong focus on addressing inequalities in business ownership.)

In a day of apps, Amazon Prime, fast food, and faster *everything*, it seems people everywhere, of every generation, are hungry to reconnect with the tangible, to see and support local businesses, creators, and makers—to slow down, even just a tad. This anthology harkens back to the days when that was the norm. When, as Talen wrote, Main Street was a daily routine, not a special visit and definitely not a tourist attraction.

Whether you've owned or worked in any aspect of a family business, helped run or maintain a small community, or have just been a loyal patron, I hope you will enjoy these essays. Thank you for reading—and for supporting a small press.

—Donna Talarico, Publisher

WHAT NEEDS DONE: THE LOVE AND BURDEN OF A FAMILY BUSINESS

MELISSA SCHOLES YOUNG

On the radio in the 1980s, between the latest hits by Richard Marx and Madonna, my eight-year-old voice told the tri-state area of Missouri, Illinois, and Iowa about our family's pest control business. Dad thought a commercial would bring in new clients who needed peanut butter glueboards and termite inspections. One night after work he brought home a tape recorder with a plug-in microphone. We stayed up late at the kitchen table rewriting our script. I learned not to breathe too much or my voice was muddled. We taped over my mistakes. I tried again and again to sound the way he wanted me to with my signature line: "When you call, tell 'em Missy sent you." My brothers mocked me every time it played on the radio, but the local celebrity was plenty.

While radio success made me a temporary sibling target, my brothers and I were raised to labor. We all wanted to be chosen to one day lead tri-state pest control domination. My liability as a girl threatened my path, but surely I could compete for a place. I answered phone calls on the business line in our house for a dime each. If a caller recognized my voice and asked me to repeat my catchphrase, I performed. I earned 10 percent commission if I convinced a new client to schedule a service. Every two weeks, I presented my itemized work invoice that added up to $3.70. Dad would round up to a $5 from his wallet. Now I know he was just teaching me math.

In a family business, every affection is laced with questions of succession, and each of us was lured to Dad's ambitions; Mom fell especially hard. Their mutual patriotism and faith in the commercialized version of the American Dream: a house, a car, money, determined our days.

My parents met when she was washing dishes at the Mark Twain Dinette, a greasy spoon in my hometown of Hannibal, Missouri. The Dinette is famous for its bathtub batch root beer and the enormous frosty mug that spins on its rooftop. Mom was fifteen years old. Her dish money helped keep her family afloat. She slept in a bed with an aunt and a sister. Four brothers shared a room next door and later, each served in the military when their turn came. Her father worked at a gas station, and her mother ran a register at JCPenney's. They were proud Catholics; every family member went to work every day and was grateful for a job. They sought order and purpose and valued time spent together in simple pleasures: growing a garden, paddling a stream, and making quilts and furniture by hand. Their American Dream was about morality rather than material success. At their house, I learned to play marbles, water (and talk to) plants, and do chores with purpose.

My parents flirted a few times in the hallway at Hannibal High School, the only secondary school in town. At the Dinette that afternoon, Dad maneuvered his convertible up to the drive-up call box and ordered a burger, fries, and chocolate milkshake. The kitchen, where Mom scrubbed grease off chili pans, was closest to the drive-up and the washers took out the orders. She knew his car and he knew where she worked. Dad offered Mom a ride home; he was waiting when her shift ended. It was a six-block ride they've made last 55 years so far.

They spent their honeymoon week in Florida hunting insects in trees and bushes for Dad's entomology class project. By then, Dad was a sophomore in college. Mom was seventeen and got pregnant quickly after they said, "I do." He quit school a few months later and returned to his father's garage for work. The garage had an apartment my parents moved into with their baby, my oldest brother. The bug class project, six display cases of pinned insects with their scientific names, hung proudly in the foyer of our business office downtown, a pest control operation they constructed over four decades from a handful of termite technicians to a tri-state success that changed the direction and economy of our lives.

Dad always says we are working class people because if we want to eat, we work. We make do. In the summer of 1982, the same year as my radio debut, we grew and harvested a mountain of corn so high that the pile's peak reached the buckles on my overalls. My brothers and I wrestled at the top of the silky cobs to be king. When the corn began to rot, we chopped and sold firewood from a flatbed truck on the side of the highway; we bred AKC German Shepherds that nobody wanted to buy; we traded the eggs from our chickens. Because they took more than they gave, we slaughtered those same chickens. Dad hammered two nails into a tree stump and stretched their necks. The chickens ran—bloody and headless—to line the banks of our pond, spilling their contents into our swimming hole. My brothers and I grabbed them by their spiny claws and dripped guts on each other's feet. Mom plucked and boiled them for dinner. I learned to be useful.

The summer I turned nine, Dad asked Mom to work for our family business; my brothers, eleven and thirteen, and I were deemed old enough to fend for ourselves alone on country roads. Dad didn't know how to turn on the new Commodore 64 computer. He needed Mom to input all customers into a database. He knew they were growing and that the computer would help them better keep track of accounts. He just didn't know how, but he knew Mom could figure it out.

Dad's father, who had run the business with his father, thought wives shouldn't work. His American Dream meant women stayed home, raised babies, read gossip magazines by the pool, and had his dinner ready when he walked through the door. He had two daughters of his own but it was only his sons who were considered for succession. He wasn't mean or rude to Mom, mostly because she behaved herself.

On her first day on the job, Mom scoured the toilet. Seven men had been sharing the one bathroom for years. No one had cleaned it, and she wasn't going to be around filth. After bleaching the toilet and adding an air freshener, she started reading the computer's instruction manual. From cover to cover. She understood they needed a bookkeeping program to manage income and expenses so she started calling accountants in the phone book. She explored the pile of cardboard boxes used to keep records. Weeks later, she suggested a file cabinet. She and Dad discussed at length how to purchase one, what it would be used for, and whether they could afford it.

Grandpa resisted change at every step. Cardboard boxes were cheaper than a filing cabinet. Hand-written sales tickets worked. It was the secretary's job to read them, not the technician's job to write clearly. Index cards held enough information for each account. Grandpa wanted to play poker, drink beer, and drive nice cars. His work day ended at 4 p.m. whether the work was done or not.

Once Mom figured out how to make the daily bank deposit, she realized there wasn't a single cent in the account to spare. She started saving 5 percent of each deposit for future taxes. She started seeing a profitable future. She wanted a plan. "We learned to save for emergencies," she said. "Trucks always need repaired, replaced, rebuilt. So do people."

On Sunday afternoons, after mass at Holy Family, we each picked our favorite donut at the grocery store across from church. Dad alternated between raspberry jelly filled and Boston crème. Mom's was a plain glazed or with almonds. My brothers just wanted chocolate anything, anything they could fight over. I chose crème horns, which only came in a four pack, another thing for my brothers to protest.

We drove our sleepy town's streets licking sugar from our fingers and staking out local businesses that did not yet patronize ours. Dad always wanted more: more business, more work, more for us. On a chalkboard in his office, he kept track of his monthly sales, set personal goals, and raised the bar with every success. Mom's job was to caution him about the unintended consequences of his wanting. "Be careful what you wish for," she warned. And she was almost always right. Dad thrived on risks, though, and more confident than his pocketbook. He peacocked at challenges. He said yes and left Mom to make it happen. And she almost always did.

As we pulled into the lots of factories and hotels that hadn't called our business for their pest control needs, Dad would park and explain how big this next job would be, how much he'd charge, how it would open doors to other business opportunities. He preached prevention rather than acute responses to pest infestations. He taught us to point through the car windows at his next conquest, again and again like we were rabid sports fans taunting the other team. Dad said our geographic closeness and intentions brought good luck and gave him the courage to put on his technician's uniform on Monday and knock on more doors.

My parents must have always hoped that business would keep the family together, but the stakes of succession cost too much. Their love story is a rags to riches one; the business of bugs was built on Midwestern grit and guts that cemented them to each other.

On the day of my college graduation, Dad made his final offer. "It ain't a bad life. There's room for you," he said. He promised an apartment, salary, and respectable office employment suitable for a girl who would never sit in the lead chair. I was dating a hometown boy who was managing the databases and computers in our office. Everything was falling into place, except me.

My older brothers were already scuttling into crawlspaces in search of termites and baiting thousands of rodent stations at the corporate clients whose parking lots we once stalked. They were each carving out territories and arguing over seating arrangements in the boardroom.

I was always leaving, though, and my belonging was never as reliable as my parent's marriage. I wanted to tell stories and majored in history in college. I listened too hard, poked too many things, and exhausted my family with my questions. My own American Dream is a struggle between my parent's striving and the moments where I learned to be still and to listen. My deepest desire is for an examined life, and I understand both the necessity and privilege of this longing. When I catch myself leaning too far forward, I settle into what I know best: the rigor of revision and the desperation of getting a sentence right. Publishing is the potential trap. There can be a relentlessness in the quest for writing success; too many targets are mobile. None of my own pursuits would have been possible without the foundation my family built. I'd return throughout my education to our family business, when I was called, to cover office maternity leaves and stock supply closets, but I never unpacked my bags again.

Decades later when I flew home from the life I've made as an academic and an author for my parents' fiftieth wedding anniversary, I organized a family dinner. We had a table at the nicest restaurant in town. It was a noticeable distance from the dirt road where we were raised. My parents had just retired or rather, they'd sold the family business to my middle brother. It is both a burden and a bequest. The passing on of generational knowledge and skill is not a step up but a leap toward wealth. When your boss is disappointed, though, it's your dad's love on the line. When you make a mistake, it costs your family most. When you do good, Mom can only offer tepid praise for fear of favoritism. An employee problem is more important that yours. The work is never done, and it seeps into every dinner conversation, every day off, and all your wishes. A family business gives and it takes. It's another sibling at the table, and there is nothing you can do to compete with it. My parents' love and teamwork made our family's business a success but it cost plenty too. Their greatest hope was that we'd have choices they didn't and that we'd never stay out of obligation.

Driving away from that celebratory family dinner I had the same painful ambiguity that I felt sitting in the front of Dad's truck, with the contents of four years of dorm life in the back. All I could see was the view out his front window and how much he'd taught me to want.

THE PERMANENCE OF ELEPHANTS

KELLY GARRIOTT WAITE

Like everything else of importance, the piano teacher's home was on Main Street. The house was small and painted a light gray and full of mystery and contradiction.

A huge magnolia tree shaded the path from the sidewalk to the three concrete steps leading to the porch. Formed into the risers of the first step and the third were identical images of a fat elephant in profile. I never knew how those elephants got there and never thought to ask. My six-year-old self imagined the elephants had been chiseled out by some former teenaged occupant of the house. But my older self—my adult self—eventually realized that was unlikely: The images were too perfect, too uniform, too deep. Perhaps a form was pressed into the concrete before it dried. Perhaps the images were carved into wet cement the way my children would—years later—use a nail to carve their initials into the newly poured floor in my father's equipment barn. I will never know the story of how they got there, but those elephants were as much a part of the piano teacher's house as the piano teacher's house was a part of Main Street.

Mom would let us off in the driveway, one of us lugging the bag of piano books. We'd climb the three stairs, grasping the black iron railing that occasionally flaked paint onto sweaty palms, and ring the bell. The front door opened into a sitting room: Inside it was cool and dark and somewhat musty. Mrs. Fitzgerald, the piano teacher, stood before us, her hair neat and elegant, her makeup flawless. She wore a skirt and blouse or a simple dress, a cloud of perfume clinging to the fabric. And always nylons and heels. "Who's first today, girls?"

The designated girl would head through the front room into the converted dining room and seat herself at the grand piano, tiny legs swinging above golden pedals. And if it was summer, the remaining sisters would head back out the front door, amid promises to return in three-quarters of an hour. Thus freed, we would turn right and walk past three houses and head into Lawson's—a convenient store popular in the area at the time. We'd reach grubby hands into our pockets to reassure ourselves of the nickels and quarters and dimes that we'd use to buy M&Ms and Reese's Peanut Butter Cups. We'd return to the front porch where we'd sit and eat our candy and watch the world go by, listening to the banging on the keyboard and the birds singing in the trees.

One year, Dr. McElliott's place—an old house converted to orthodontic purposes—was torn down. Built in its place was a two-story building sided in cedar. I resented that building for its newness; for the fact of its two stories in a one-story town; for the beauty of its new siding. But over the years, the building weathered and turned gray, and eventually, the townspeople adopted it as theirs.

The first floor held a dress shop. And when we deemed ourselves of sufficient age, my sisters and I began venturing down the walk and inside to the air-conditioned shop where we would paw with chocolate-covered fingers through endless racks of dresses, pretending to be customers. Of course, we fooled no one but ourselves, believing that we'd succeeded in duping the shopkeeper who followed stealthily behind us, inquiring every so often as to whether we *required assistance.*

And, when it was time, we'd return to the house of the piano teacher to exchange roles; one of us taking a seat at the piano bench, one of us heading outside into the heat of the day to join her sister at Lawson's or perhaps the dress shop.

Winters, we took refuge on the red velvet loveseat that was pressed against the windows of the front room of the piano teacher's house. I would run my thumbnail against the grain of the fabric, drawing pictures in velvet, listening to my sister's warm-up scales. On the table to the right, there was a wooden box, which I felt entitled to open. Inside there were dried rose petals—yellow—that must have held some great significance for the piano teacher. But I considered them only for their entertainment value as I opened the box, inhaled the memory of scent, and thoughtlessly poked a tiny index finger into fragile recollections.

On the coffee table in front of the velvet loveseat, there was all manner of magazines: *Woman's Day*, *McCall's*, even the scandalous *Cosmopolitan*... and it was this magazine that presented the first contradiction: How could such a proper woman—a woman whose constant uniform was a dress and nylons and heels, a woman whose first name was Evelyn, a woman who loved Beethoven and Mozart and Liszt—have any interest in *Cosmopolitan*? No matter. I studied those magazines intently, wondering whether *this marriage could be saved* and reading serialized fiction, paying particular attention to the photographs and the saucier articles in *Cosmo*.

To the left of the red velvet couch, there was a recliner—green vinyl. And next to that recliner was an ashtray on a tall stand, as out of place as my sisters and I looked in the dress shop down the street. Perhaps in deference to Mrs. Fitzgerald's sensibilities, the ashtray was gold. It had a lid, also gold, and a black push button that spun the lid around and down, winging the ash off the lid and into the hidden depths below. Every week, the ashtray was clean and new, and I would pass a few minutes pushing the black button, watching the lid spin and descend before rising again.

The last chair in the room had lace doilies along the back and arms and a needlepoint footstool in front. This chair belonged to the piano teacher's mother, Mrs. Timbley: an ancient woman with watery eyes behind bifocals. She was shortish and fattish and had a head full of tight white curls. Mrs. Timbley would slowly come down the dark wooden stairs, grasping tightly to the heavy banister. "Hello, girls," she would say, sighing gently into her chair and waiting for her daughter to bring her a cup of coffee.

Sometime in the middle of the second lesson, the piano teacher's husband would arrive home from work wearing his blue coveralls. "Afternoon!" he would roar.

"Oh, Bud." Mrs. Fitzgerald would look up and give a disciplinary frown.

He'd stomp into the kitchen with his big black lunchbox, then head to his bedroom, the stairs protesting beneath his heavy tread. A few moments later, he would descend again, wearing his at-home uniform: jeans, a tee-shirt, and always a cigar. Mr. Fitzgerald was loud to his wife's quiet. He was large to her small. In his own gentle way, he was rough. He'd sit in his recliner and call to the hound dog, who would jump into his lap. And while he rubbed that dog's ears, Mr. Fitzgerald would talk to us about life.

And if an ambulance or a fire truck should happen to pass by on Main, that old hound dog would leap from Mr. Fitzgerald's lap and onto the red velvet loveseat. He'd put his paws on the backrest, raise his head to the sky and howl piteously. Mr. Fitzgerald would laugh and Mrs. Fitzgerald would frown merrily and my sisters and I would cover our ears and smile.

When I was summoned to my lesson, I would smooth down the drawing in the red velvet couch and rise to my feet.

◆

Our first piano was a basement piano: an ugly old upright painted thick with orange. Many of its teeth were chipped; some were missing their enamel altogether, and on these keys, someone had penciled in their names: C...D...E

Once a day, I'd go down the basement steps, gray with black stick-on treads and cross the orange tiled floor and seat myself at that old piano, fully intending to practice. But instead, I'd find myself pretending I was the piano player at the Silver Dollar Saloon in Bonanza—banging the keys on that upright mercilessly without regard for sound or rhythm. I'd end my performance in a magnificent glissando covering the entire span of white keys before spinning around on my bench to face my invisible audience—the ping pong table, too—for the thunderous applause that only I could hear.

And then my mother's voice would float down the stairs. "Is that your lesson?"

Well, no. It wasn't. But it was a whole lot more interesting than *A Dozen a Day* and *Scales and Chords are Fun.*

My sisters and I pursued this lackluster approach to our lessons as long as we could, gamely faking our way through our weekly lessons, occasionally causing the old hound dog to howl at our efforts. And then one day, we were invited to the piano teacher's house for tea.

Oh, how lovely, I probably thought. *Mrs. Fitzgerald enjoys us so much, she'd like to have us to tea.*

The table was set. The tea was poured. The cookies were set upon a plate. The piano teacher's mother and husband were nowhere to be seen. Even the dog had seemingly disappeared. I was too pleased with myself to be suspicious. I felt suddenly grown up, sitting there, drinking tea—real tea—out of fancy cups with saucers. And then Mrs. Fitzgerald, petite, *gentle* Mrs. Fitzgerald began to lecture. "You know," she began, sweetly enough, blowing upon her tea. "Your parents work hard to send you to these lessons."

I set down my tea. The liquid suddenly tasted bitter.

"And you're not keeping up your end of the bargain." She stared intently at each of us in turn.

"But..."

"But nothing."

I pushed away my tea. I refused to eat my cookies. I would punish Mrs. Fitzgerald with my steely gaze.

"I cannot continue to teach you girls if you're unwilling to practice. I can't take your parents' good money."

Within five minutes, she had the three of us in tears. Our tea grew cold in the pretty cups. The cookies were ignored.

I hated Mrs. Fitzgerald that day. But the three of us practiced long and hard that week, and we continued to practice long and hard until we were back in her good graces again.

And, I'm happy to report, we were never invited to tea again.

◆

The piano teacher's bathroom was at the top of the stairs and, of course, each week, I would have to use it—if only to break up the monotony of waiting for my piano lesson. I would climb the wooden staircase, stepping lightly, hoping to have a peek into the room to the right.

This room belonged to the piano teacher's mother and, invariably, the door would be open. The room was dominated by a massive bed—a bed so high, a stepping stool stood sentry at its side. The bedspread was white as snow. The bed itself was of a dark ancient wood. It looked so inviting in its size and softness, it was all I could do to keep myself from entering the room, from climbing that stool and sitting upon the bed.

I would have liked to explore that house—to open up doors and cabinets, to peek inside things in order to gain a bit more insight into the lives of Mrs. Fitzgerald, her husband, and her mother. But the other upstairs doors were closed, and I didn't dare open them.

There were beautiful soaps in the bathroom: tiny decorative soaps that fit into the palm of my hand. They looked—and smelled—like various flowers, and I wondered why we didn't have these soaps at home. A tiny hand towel was set out for drying and, looking back, I wonder how the piano teacher's husband felt about the flower soaps and the tiny towels.

As the years passed, Mrs. Timbley came downstairs for her coffee less frequently. Eventually, she stopped coming down altogether. On my trips to the bathroom, I would see her tucked into bed, her glasses folded neatly upon the nightstand. She slept so soundly; she looked so peaceful with the covers drawn up beneath her chin that I would conclude that she had died. Then, frightened, I would hurry into the bathroom and back down the stairs barely taking the time to admire the pretty soaps in the dish.

But it was the piano teacher's husband who died, unexpectedly felled at work by a heart attack. Because my mother said it was *the right thing to do*, we went to the calling hours. I hovered close to my mother, casting nervous glances at the man I once knew lying in a coffin at the front of the room. The piano teacher was a different woman. She was shrunken, weighted down by her sadness. Her pasted-on smile threatened to crack and break. And, then, when she saw us huddled there, waiting to pay our respects, it did. She embraced each of us in turn and thanked us for coming and then, Mrs. Fitzgerald, that pillar of strength, that giver of stern tea-parties, broke down in tears. That day, Mrs. Fitzgerald became less of a piano teacher to me and more of a person: a person, yes, of strength. But also, a person of weakness and needs and tragedy.

Piano lessons were suspended for a time, but eventually, we returned to that red velvet couch where I'm sure it pained Mrs. Mrs. Fitzgerald to see that empty green vinyl chair, to hear that old hound dog howl piteously whenever an ambulance went by.

As time went on and my mother learned she was pregnant with my brother, my parents bought some property and built a house and a barn in another town. The old house was packed and patched up and painted for the new owners.

But we left that old upright right where it stood. It had taken four laughing men to haul that orange piano to our basement. Mom and Dad decided to leave it behind. We got a new piano teacher and a new piano—a gorgeous baby grand that held court in the living room.

I'm sure Mrs. Fitzgerald is long dead, but I wish that I could see her one last time to thank her and to tell her that I learned a lot more than just music from her. I learned about duty and expectations and struggling with money. I learned about truth and honesty. I learned that sometimes a parent depends upon a child. I learned how to speak to older people; people who weren't related to me. And I learned that opposites sometimes *do* attract. But most of all, I learned that love—a love of music, a love of family, a love for a piano teacher, a love for an old forgotten town—can be as permanent as a pair of elephants etched in concrete.

REFLECTIONS ON MY GRANDMOTHER'S COSTUME SHOP WHILE ANXIOUSLY MAKING MASKS

MELISSA HART

Step 1. Cut two fabric rectangles, 6 ½" by 9 ½", for the mask. Cut four fabric strips, 1" by 16", for straps. The scissors are Fiskars, the only brand my grandmother would ever touch. A bouquet of them bloomed, orange-handled, in a jar beside her sewing machine at home. Weekends, I fled my college dormitory with its endless margarita parties and slept on the daybed in her sewing room next to the dressmaker's bust, size 12, and the plastic bins marked "sequins," "fringe," and "faux fur."

Once, I had to hoist a full-length gorilla costume from the bed and drape it on a door hook. Other evenings, I exhumed Egyptian togas or Renaissance dresses heavy with embroidery and glass jewels. The masks on the top of high cabinets—a Chewbacca head in for repairs, a terrifying foam-and-cardboard Easter bunny head—gave me dreams so vivid and strange that I'd awake unsure of both where I was and *who* I was.

Whole minutes, I blinked at the weak coastal sunlight streaming in from the window and illuminating the silver blades of the Fiskars. Ronald Reagan had just passed his torch to George H.W. Bush. AIDS was ravaging the country, and my older brother—a chef in upstate New York—had succumbed to the disease. Outside the sewing room door, my grandmother's slippers tapped; I imagined her thick fingers twitching to get to her sewing.

Step 2. Fold in raw edges; sew straps down the middle. Pin straps in the corners of one rectangle. Place other rectangle on top, and pin with right sides together. My own thick fingers fumble with the pins, ancient and rusty, stuck into a three-lobed pincushion that must once have resembled a flower and now boasts the color and texture of a cat's hairball long after the expulsion.

My grandmother grew up in the Great Depression, daughter of circus performers turned vaudeville comics and jugglers. When she was a toddler, they lost her for hours. An acrobat finally discovered her napping in the elephant barn.

Her parents were also aviators; summers, she flew with them from theater to theater on her mother's lap in a biplane painted with their show business names. The rest of the year, they abandoned her to a great aunt in Kansas City so she could attend school. On the family farm, 90 miles north, a trio of other aunts taught her to sew crazy quilts—heavy blankets made from worn-out clothing scraps and pieced together with wild, multicolored chicken-scratch embroidery.

My grandmother graduated high school and worked for a time as a secretary, then married a fastidious and exacting World War II soldier who left off commanding liberty ships and commenced commanding her and their two small daughters. She was not allowed to work. They were not allowed to cough. For years, he bound my mother's left arm to her chest, telling her southpaws were the work of Satan.

This was the early 1950s. My grandmother had no savings, no home of her own. She was stuck, pinned in a beautiful house in the hills above the

Monterey coast. She was allowed to volunteer as a costume seamstress for a community theater company on Fisherman's Wharf; she never dreamed that those first silk and satin assignments would change her whole life.

Step 3. Sew around the perimeter of the mask, ½" from the edges, leaving a 2" gap on one side. Turn the mask right side out. My grandmother's sewing box is round brown wicker embroidered with faded pink roses. In it, a jumble of old needles and stitch-rippers and stray rhinestones and gold tassels, along with her smallest Fiskars sharp enough to cut to the truth of any matter.

After her parents retired from their work as U.S.O. entertainers and moved to Monterey themselves, her mother shook her head at the domestic disaster my grandmother had gotten herself into. "I raised you to live in a big world," she said. "What the hell are you doing with your life?"

My grandmother filed for divorce. She became a single mother, purchased a building on Lighthouse Road with a check from her parents, and opened up a costume shop. These weren't the cheap paper and plastic outfits bought in drugstores the day before Halloween for ten dollars; they were handmade, hundreds of them, researched from history books and pop culture magazines and sewn by machine in an alcove between the shop's lobby and the dressing room.

An actor from the Wharf Theater—former hoofer in MGM musicals—purchased the space adjoining hers and opened up a dance studio. Together, they ran the "Theatre Dance Showcase" just up the street from the ocean, and turned it into Monterey's go-to location for tap and ballet lessons—and costumes for Halloween and Christmas-in-July-parties and masquerades. They maintained their properties and their romance for 40 years. Each time he proposed, she refused to marry him. He could stay every night in the beautiful house with her and her girls, but she would never again commit herself for life. She would, however, host endless parties with him—sparkling costumed affairs for their cohort of friends from community theaters, dance companies, and the local art gallery

Step 4. Pin three folds on the front of the mask. Topstitch all around, ½" from the edges. My grandmother owned numerous sewing machines over years. She left me the last one, a five-stitch Singer. A few years before she purchased it, her father had built a homemade airplane in his backyard to fly over the Salinas Valley. He took it up with a younger pilot, and the plane exploded midair. After the funeral, my great-grandmother moved in. She established herself at one corner of the kitchen table and began sewing crazy quilts while my grandmother sewed at her shop.

On road trips to Monterey in my mother's VW bus, we stopped at the costume shop and greeted my grandmother at her sewing machine beside a glass display case of fake mustaches and latex cigars and false eyelashes, and the pièce de résistance—a battery-operated light saber before anyone else had them. She embraced me awkwardly, with a bemused groan instead of a kiss, and then I was free to try on her costumes.

Racks of them lined the back room, organized by era. Leopard-print loincloths and latex caveman-clubs hung at the start, progressing through Cleopatra sheaths and Renaissance gowns and capes, and Victorian hoop skirts and pioneer calico, and roaring twenties flappers and poodle skirts, all the way up to aliens and Chewbacca and a white Princess Leia dress complete with a dual-bun wig.

In costume, I slipped into the empty dance studio and paraded past the wall of mirrors. In the next room, sounds of the sewing machine—bursts of stitching and anxious conversation between my grandmother and my mother.

My mother left my abusive father and came out as a lesbian in 1979, losing custody of me in a homophobic courtroom in a homophobic county down south. My grandmother took orders for Smurf costumes and Ninja Turtles; she bemoaned kids and their gum, adults and their cigarettes, declared the weeks before and after Halloween her own personal hell. And still, she sewed.

Step 5. Iron the mask, pressing folds down firmly. I inherited my grandmother's iron, as well: broken on one side and revealing the inner workings of the machine. When I was 30, a stage four cancer diagnosis elicited my grandmother's bemused groan. With our family around her hospital bed and no costumes in sight, she performed an E.T. puppet show with the red-lit pulse monitor on her index finger.

In the years since I'd graduated from college, she'd witnessed the death of her mother at the kitchen table, and the dissolution of her 40-year romance with the actor. She'd watched her younger daughter collect DUIs like others collected abalone shells washed up on the Monterey beach and flee the state to drink in obscurity elsewhere. She closed the costume shop and sold the building to a new owner who turned it into a Cheesecake Factory. She sold her beautiful house, as well, and left her artsy cohort of friends and moved to Southern California to live close to me and my mother. "I've always wanted an English garden," she said of her tiny front yard collection of flowers, mentioning nothing about the half-acre of blossoms and fruit trees she'd left behind in Monterey. She chose a sunny alcove in her new house, surrounded by backyard roses, to become her sewing room, and then her hospice room.

You do the work you know how to do until you can't do it anymore, she told me, regardless of what life throws at you. You provide entertainment where you can.

She left me her sewing machine and her iron. I listen to the news with its terrifying reports of COVID-19-related illnesses and deaths. Masks can save us, infectious disease doctor Anthony Fauci insists. Most stores don't yet carry them. The ones that do have sold out. I find a pattern online, turn off the news, and set up the ironing board. Action is solace, especially when it leads to protecting my family and friends. I sew.

CANDY IS STRONG WHEN THE MARROW IS SWEET

DYANN NASHTON

Mention turkey joints to the uninitiated, and noses turn up. But Turkey Joints—proper noun—are neither smoked nor floating in a jar of pink-tinged liquid at the butcher. This confectionery novelty is a local delicacy in my hometown. Bite through the silvery candy shell and you'll come upon a silky marrow of chocolate and nuts. The combination of crunchy crispness and creamy center is irresistible and addictive.

Each individual Turkey Joint is the length of a hand. You buy them by the jar at a price that rivals a really good bottle of wine. The candy is in season only during the holidays. It is *hygroscopic*, meaning that it absorbs moisture, so Upstate New York's humidity halts production in the summer. Best eaten fresh, they're the ideal gift for a hostess or someone who has everything, more thoughtful than an elaborate fruit basket and far superior to a potted poinsettia wrapped in cheap, colored foil. Ceremoniously brought out after Christmas dinner, Turkey Joints are often presented on a dish, glistening like icicles. Children instinctively reach for the candy much as they reach for a fragile, prized ornament on the tree, and—in both cases—their hands are routinely swatted away.

Rome, New York, would never be confused with Hershey, Pennsylvania. Once a major transportation hub during the settlement of the colonies and western expansion, it now has boarded-up schools. On the other side of the tracks, grand old homes are divided reluctantly into apartments. Dutch elm disease killed seventy-five percent of the old elms that arched to meet each over the streets that ran North to South. Kids break into rusted skeleton buildings to build bike ramps or smoke pot. After manufacturing died, our downtown disintegrated with urban renewal. Then, the military base closed, and some of Rome's soul went with it.

But we had Turkey Joints.

The candy was made mainly by Tasos—my Uncle Tasi. His name, short for Anastassios, meant *resurrection* in Greek. As family legend has it, he lived up to his name at least once by surviving as a prisoner of war during World War II. Then he became part of one of Greece's biggest exports at that time—an immigrant. He boarded a ship to the United States and didn't look back.

Uncle Tasi and Aunt Nora made their home and the Turkey Joints on Doxtator Street, which began at a commercial two-lane boulevard and ended at Embargo Street. The front of the house appeared no different than any other aluminum-clad ranch home in that part of town, but it was the only one with an owner-occupied business. It faced a row of bland duplexes relocated there from the once-growing air force base.

A porch out back was winterized and finished, leaving one interior wall still covered in siding and an occasional window covered over with painted wood to make shelves. Linoleum floors met faux-wood paneled walls. That is where the candy was made.

I was 14 when I started working in the Turkey Joint factory, just one of the rotating four or five friends and relatives who helped out when needed.

The day started at 7 a.m. and ended once ten good batches of candy were completed. Sometimes that was around five, and at other times, it pushed into evenings. Customers refused to leave when we ran out, so we stayed and made more.

On my first day, Aunt Nora asked where my slippers were. Shaking her head, she came back into the room with a fabric pair, rubber-soled and two sizes too big for me. "You can't wear your sneakers on the floor," she tsked. Outdoor shoes were unsanitary going into the work floor and fractured bits of sugar could stick to the bottoms and be tracked into the adjoining house on the way out. In addition to our slippers, we each donned a crisp, white apron and tied it at our waists. Aunt Nora pushed a hairnet at me. I looked at it, at everybody else, and pulled it over my head, flattening the hair-sprayed curls I'd worked hard on that morning.

My uncle drove a truck more than an hour north to Fulton to get the chocolate from Nestlé—what locals there called the "chocolate works." The entire city near Lake Ontario smelled of cocoa. The unmistakable fragrance carried from Uncle Tasi's truck into the workspace. In the first room the chocolate was melted in a giant copper cauldron and stirred with a wooden paddle. Flames heated a resin that smelled like cotton candy. The atmosphere was sweet and delectable, like working inside a big soothing cup of hot cocoa. Cardboard cartons of Brazil nuts were neatly stacked. Three or four 100-pound sacks of sugar bulged on top of one another.

Sensitive and temperamental molten sugar was poured and kneaded into submission in the second room. It was cooler by design and we watched my uncle work while waiting for our call to action. Tools meant for giants lived there: machete-like knives, a huge hook on the wall, and scissors that took two hands to operate. The knives were used to scrape hardening sugar on marble or stainless steel tables. Gelatinous sugar masses were pulled over the hook like taffy.

Sometimes the candy didn't cooperate, and my uncle's Greek blood reddened his face. "Somonabeach!" was followed by an assortment of Greek expletives. He had a high voice for a large, strong man. Those gargantuan tools would fly from his leather gloves across the room. We ducked behind the counters then stayed late for the do-over batch.

Big blobs of uncongealed sugar were manipulated on the table and then on the hook as it cooled. Uncle Tasi's muscular brown arms worked in a fluid rhythm. At the far end of the large room stood a heated contraption with conveyor belts that he would labor over to stretch the candy to perfection. The rest of us spent our day several feet away in the smaller room to the right, an intentional afterthought.

Aunt Nora took her post by the scale on the counter. We hovered, waiting around a big circular cooling tray, a fine-meshed screen within a wooden frame. The candy came down the chute from the conveyor belts and we gingerly spread them on the tray. We'd press a little, glowing doorbell button to let Uncle Tasi know that we'd filled a tray. He would stop the conveyor belt so we could lift the tray and set it aside then move on to the next.

All the while Uncle Tasi—at 5'11" with a big belly—hunched over the work surface, painstakingly wrestling a glob of hot candy. A few small gas flames gave him a bit more time to get it just so before sending the shiny rope slithering down the conveyor belts. Every so often he would lean away from the candy and over to someone posted by his side, as if he had a one-word secret or joke. She would wipe his brow and face with a soft white folded cloth.

I was eventually promoted, earning the added responsibility of wiping Uncle Tasi's sweat so that it couldn't sting his eyes or—worse—drip in the candy. I've told that story often, proudly. When reminiscing with a cousin in recent years, he laughed. "Yeah, we let you think that was a promotion."

The little bone-shaped candies, glossy and fragile, cooled and hardened around the molten chocolate fingers on the trays. We carefully slid them into the jars, the distinctive green and gold embossed Turkey Joints label already affixed. Aunt Nora weighed the jars. A sheet of thin emerald waxed paper was wound around the top of the opening to keep the candy secure. There was an art to efficiently winding-nestling the paper in there. Metal lids screwed on top.

"Tasos!" Aunt Nora yelled to the bigger room. Her voice was surprisingly rich for her tiny stature and delicately featured face. "Your niece is workin' for the public here!" she announced, surgically extracting one or two pieces from the overweight jar. Getting those knobby, fragile joints to all stand up straight at attention was like a puzzle; sometimes just the right skinny or fat one would make the others fall in line. It was more difficult getting them back out.

Expensive and exquisite, the Turkey Joints would glow inside their cylindrical glass displays. Customers would hold them up, turning the jar back and forth to admire their sheen.

One December, we all went home wilted and late for Christmas Eve dinner. We needed several additional batches to keep up with demand. Customers that year complained that the chocolate on the inside of the candy was still runny.

No one wants to rush through a jar. But it's a bad idea to squirrel them away or save them for a special occasion. Over time, it can lose its sheen and become tacky and anemic in contrast to its brilliant metallic label. The lifespan of a Turkey Joint illustrates the lesson of using the fine china, the good linens, now.

It was normal for about six or seven pounds of candy to be lost at the beginning and end of each batch and there was always some breakage. In my first year of high school, I became rather popular at lunchtime, as kids loved reaching into the plastic bag smeared inside with dried chocolate for Turkey Joint rejects and jagged pieces. We were all allowed to take some home, a fringe benefit. Today, a 12-ounce bag of these tidbits sells for $11.49.

The job consumed my weekends until after the holidays when things slowed and my social life improved. I moved on to other part-time jobs, like waitressing and being a radio announcer, and soon learned that outside of a family business, spinning that one silvery sugar thread can be elusive. Everything has its process. Supplies need to be fetched. An ideal climate maintained and late nights sacrificed. There is the right way to do things, and there are broken pieces and bad batches. All are easier to endure when it's family by your side.

At Uncle Tasi's funeral, a sense of loss struck me for the first time. I stood with family at the graveside. Grief stung and was embarrassing, as tears washed down my cheeks and my nose drained over my lip. I hadn't spent time with him or helped with the Turkey Joints in years. He gave me my first job. His name meant resurrection. I did not have a tissue to stanch the tears for the uncle whose brow I'd wiped. But the candy and the memories remain, and both are sweet.

ON THE CORNER OF ATLANTIC AND OSBORNE

LINDSAY GELAY-AKINS

We pulled weeds with screwdrivers. Phillips-head or flat, it didn't matter.

We sealed envelopes with our sandpaper tongues.

When we finally learned our ABCs we could file invoices, but the cabinets were high and if you weren't keen enough to choose the right tool for a boost (it seemed everything always had to be filed in the top drawer) you could end up face-planting into the top of the filing cabinet. Although useful, a rolly chair is a precarious means to elevation. We learned pretty quickly that a few boxes of brake pads or fuel injectors stacked neatly—and sturdily—atop one another were a better choice. It's amazing how devoid of permanent injury we are considering the years worth of balancing experiments and envelope licking we did.

We learned how to sort washers by the subtle differences in their circumferences, sizes, and thicknesses. We learned how to degrit our fingernails, our shoes, our clothes. We learned how to get the grease to come off our hands as easily as the spring dew evaporates in the sunlight.

We also learned how best to fold pizza slices to capture all the cheese we possibly could in one bite. We learned where the best hiding spots were among the endless rows of mufflers in the garage. We learned how to venture down the creaky staircase and sneak onto the loading dock without being seen or heard. We learned how to make copies of our own hands in funny shapes on the Xerox machine.

Amidst our weed pulling, our envelope licking, our endless games of hide-and-seek, and our limitless laughter we learned about the value of hard work. We learned about the value of having a father who provided for us. We learned about the value of family.

◆

When my great-grandfather, August, started the business, I doubt he ever imagined it would become what it is today. He spent his days traveling up and down New Jersey selling refined oil to anyone who would buy it. The demand was fair. It was 1949, and wealthy and middle-class families were itching for a car of their own. And those cars—and the garages and gas stations that serviced them—needed oil. World War II was a distant memory and the economy had been maintaining its peri-war momentum. The timing was right.

August devoted decades of his life to oil sales and the venture was profitable enough, but when it came time to retire he must have felt the potency of his pursuits beginning to wane. He was ready to pass along this business he created to his son, my grandfather, Thomas, but the exchange ushered in unique complexities. Papers had to be drawn up. Lawyers hired. Signatures inked.

Egos clashed. My great-grandfather refused to pass on his business without a signed testament that his eldest son would care for him and his family for the rest of their lives. My grandfather, a vernal 19-year-old, agreed and painfully accepted the unsavory realization that his father didn't trust he would be cared for by his first-born son without legal guarantee.

The labor of my great-grandfather became that of my grandfather, but for Thomas the business was so much more than just selling oil. He eventually acquired a warehouse and began to lightly stock oil filters and other automobile necessities. When a property opened up in the quaint but bustling beach town of Manasquan, New Jersey, he bought the building and created a storefront. It was 1969. The year of Woodstock. The year we put a man on the moon. The year of the Pontiac Firebird Trans Am. The year of Hi-Way Oil Service's conception.

There was less than $1,000 to spare and $25,000 worth of stock in the shop that needed to be paid off in a month's time. The road ahead looked riddled with potholes, but Thomas was undaunted. Profit was closer than anyone had imagined, and within a year Hi-Way Oil Service was thriving with the strength of a long-established investment.

My grandfather spent his days on the road selling auto parts to mechanics, garages, and gas stations. He hustled. He networked. He kept the business viable beyond the four walls of the store while his brother forged relationships with customers from behind the shop's counter. My grandfather had a high school diploma and a hardy work ethic. No college degree. No MBA. Not even a hint of formal post-secondary education, and yet business boomed under his leadership.

In 2000, my father and his brother inherited the business when my grandfather finally retired. (Although even at 89, he spends his days sorting through boxes and categorizing parts—much to my father's chagrin.) My uncle inherited my grandfather's role as the traveling salesman, and my father stepped into his uncle's role as the counterman. It's a system that has continued for several decades.

Seventy years of sweat, oil, and grease form the foundation of my family's success. Seventy years of service to private enterprises, to public companies, to our family. And when it comes to the business, age doesn't matter. The only thing that matters is your work ethic. If you want to be at the shop, you have to earn the right to be there. And each of us—every child, every grandchild, every great-grandchild—is still a minute cog in the machine that keeps the business running.

◆

When I was young—weed-picking-with-screwdrivers young, not invoice-filing young—my father had the company insignia on the east facade of the building repainted. The red, black, and yellow pigments stretched ten feet up; they were saturated with pride and longevity. A shining beacon of generations of modest and grueling work. A testament to the good ‘ol Blue Collar Toil.

Customers were loyal then. Not yet bought by AutoZone or Amazon. They honored their unspoken contracts and relied on my father to deliver on their newest desires; to fulfill their every need.

“You got a head gasket for an ’84 Mustang?”

“Not on me,” my dad would say. “I'll order it and have it here for you by tomorrow morning.”

And that's how business was. Not business. Service.

◆

Sometime during my childhood, a candy salesman convinced my father to get one of those dispensers with gumballs and M&Ms and Mike-and-Ikes. The candy was never free (until my future-engineer brother eventually figured out how to jimmy the levers). The machine took quarters, and the only way to get quarters around the shop was to earn them. So we picked weeds. We washed windows. We stacked empty boxes. No job was too menial when it came to earning a handful of candy. When my father opened the cash register to retrieve the coins we knew that our labor was worthy of praise. We ate into his profits, but we feasted like kings on those chewy sweets. Our hard work paid dividends in a myriad of glorious flavors and, of course, in countless cavities.

◆

My love of books was forged in the upstairs office amid coffee-stained ledgers and the printing calculator's steady staccato. The office had dark brown, faux wood grain, laminate-paneled walls and it was where my father did all the accounting for the business. There was no need to hire a professional. He knew how to add and subtract, so he was easily able to determine profit and loss. Being self-sufficient and confident is how the men in my family built—and continue to build—their empire. Decades worth of their determination and grit settled deeply into those walls and it seeped out into all of us as we grew up.

In the office, the numbers weren't what interested me. It was the potential for my words to be written down and bound that kept me in there for hours. Among the drab decor, reams of paper—and not just white paper, but pastel yellow, pink, and blue—glowed like radiant flares against a night sky on a dusty, browning bookshelf. The colored paper was reserved for the front and back covers of my self-published literature, while the stark white sheets made up the meaty middle pages.

I spent endless afternoons at my father's flesh-beige formica desk, adjacent to my uncle's and grandfather's workstations, trying to figure out how to secure the bindings of my books to make them look "real." My palms wore shiny divots into the desktop. My fingers bled when I stapled my skin by accident. The tightly woven brown carpet was dented from the frantic footfalls that brought me from desk to desk in search of just the right tools. Nothing could stop me in my pursuit to create the most flawless book spine possible. During those long days of laboring I learned about the importance of persistence and creativity. No one taught me these values. No one had to. They were, and are, just part of the tapestry of the shop.

My books are still there and so are the old ledgers. They reside in the top drawer of my father's desk. They safely guard my childhood innocence.

◆

Every Christmas my father decorated the large picture windows that lined the front of the store with mechanical Santas and those three-foot-tall plastic light-up candles. They had that made-in-the-70s smell. The true scent of nostalgia. He'd spray snow from a can along the edges of the windows to create festive scenes of elves holding radiator fluid or windshield wipers.

When he was finally finished, my brother, mother, and I would pile into the car and go down to the shop to stand and stare in awe at his latest holiday creation. Passers-by would lessen their pace to admire the festive display. At night, cars would slow in the glow of the twinkling lights to enjoy the view. Those windows were perfect. Priceless. Because my dad had made them. Because he had Rudolph jumping on a stack of steering wheel covers. Because these windows, just like the shop itself, were made for us.

◆

Every new decade seemed to require yet another adjustment. In the '80s it was new profit margins. In the '90s it was a total rebranding. At the turn of the century, it was transitioning from carbon paper to internet connections. Computers replaced the paper catalog systems that housed part numbers. Their bulk began to obstruct the customer-salesman connection forged from across the counter. They required extension cords and software. Keyboards and CPUs. The men in my family had to adapt to a new era of buying and selling: automation, PINs, pull-down menus, codes. It was all the same business wrapped up in a new package. As the computers and their ever-changing software needs moved in, the invoices of my childhood moved out, along with the mufflers that were quickly sold or scrapped to make room for a skilled mechanic willing to rent the garage space and the adjoining metal shop for a fair price.

The windows became bare. "Too much work," my dad would growl.

The sign on the east facade began to fade and so did the luster of serving customers.

"Well I can get this at Walmart for 40 cents less," they would gripe.

So, it was either take the hit and sell the parts at cost or tell John—who promised decades ago that our shop was the best in the business and that he'd never stray—to take a damn hike. Either way, my father had to forfeit something. It was his livelihood or his sanity.

◆

I was chest-deep in my last semester of grad school writing my thesis and studying for my Comps, but I found time to visit for the weekend, and, of course, I stopped by the shop. I had to make copies; my bank account no longer afforded visits to Staples.

While rummaging through my father's dust-laden desk for a decent pen and some Wite-Out, I found it. It was haphazardly stashed next to all of my faded school pictures. A birthday card. But clearly a keepsake. The front read, "Farting is an art..."

I snickered to myself. A fart joke. Whoever gave this to my father knew him well.

The inside said, "Happy Birthday, Rembrandt!"

I smiled. What an accurate sentiment. Simple. Easy. Funny. Happy. Just like my dad. My eyes scrolled down past the "I love you!" but I didn't recognize the signature. It was the handwriting of someone I'd never heard of. A woman I had never met.

I placed the card back in the desk drawer and sat back in the rolly chair. It's rusted wheels creaked under me. I stared at the carpet. How did it become so faded? So grey. I saw specks of dirt shoot straight into the air like miniature missiles as I moved the toe of my shoe against the fibers, unsure of my next move.

I left without the Wite-Out and with a stack of useless copies. On the way to my car, I passed the east façade. The sign was so faded it nearly disappeared into the background.

◆

The warehouse on the second floor of the shop used to be full of supplies. There were infinite rows of carburetors, catalytic converters, brake light bulbs, and jumper cables. But as the shelves slowly emptied they were replaced not with more merchandise, but with boxes bursting with mementos from my childhood. My American Girl doll. My art pieces from 5th grade. My photo albums from high school. Souvenirs from family vacations. The slatted wooden floor was covered with workout equipment from our family home that had long-since been sold—collateral damage of my parent's divorce. It all sits there now. Dusty. Rusting. A representation of life before.

◆

As I emerged into adulthood, visits to the shop became infrequent. I only stopped by if I wanted to locate a distant memory stored away in one of my boxes or if I needed new wiper blades. I never stayed long. I never knew what I might find if I did. I never made another book or searched for another pen. I bought my own printer.

I'd grown, but nothing about the shop changed. Parts were still ordered and sorted. Profits and losses were still calculated. Deliveries were still made. Desks were still dusty, pictures were still fading, and cards were still stored in desk drawers.

◆

One midsummer day my husband and I were returning home from a local petting zoo with our two children. We weren't far from the shop. (No one ever is.)

"Let's stop and see your dad," my husband suggested.

"I don't know," I hesitated. "We just got the kids cleaned up. I don't want them to get all dirty again."

He rolled his eyes, "Come on. Your dad will love it."

I navigated the traffic circle pointing our truck in the direction of the store. "Fine," I acquiesced. "But not too long."

When we arrived my father lit up. "Hey! What are you guys doing here?"

"Just coming for a visit," I replied.

My father lifted my daughter out of her car seat. She clung to him, happy to see her grandfather; it was the same delight I felt when seeing my own grandfather all those years ago during visits to the shop. The afternoon passed in fits of laughter. Climbing on boxes. Putting old golf balls into the cobwebbed corners of shelves. Running on the pocky concrete floor through stacks of brake fluid and WD-40.

All the while my father answered phones, scheduled deliveries, helped customers replace their wiper blades and headlights, and typed complex codes into his most up-to-date organizational software. The hustle never stops, it just changes form.

I looked to the corner where the candy machine used to be. Now there's a wall of washers, half full. "I think you need to order some supplies over here," I commented, gesturing toward the sad display of goods.

"Nah," my dad answered. "No one buys that stuff from me anymore."

Not when Home Depot has a wider selection at a more consumer-satisfying price.

I wondered briefly why he left it up. Before I could ask, a collage of old photographs stole my attention. I searched through the faces and happened upon a picture of my grandfather when his hair was still an ashy brown, standing on a newly glossed, blue concrete floor. There were pictures of me with my grandparents at a shop Christmas party. There were so many faces of family members and customers I didn't recognize and would never meet. My brother, my cousins, and my aunts and uncles were all up there, their smiles suspended in time. As I perused each snapshot I recalled to my husband: "Grandpa used to make us pull weeds out front with screwdrivers."

He laughed.

"It was very effective," I said as I smiled.

The thought of my sweat being part of the equity entombed in this place made me wonder if my great-grandfather ever could have anticipated that his grease-stained fingernails and his sweaty brow helped create the space that allowed his family to bloom. But I suppose that was never his goal. He wanted to provide for his family in the best way he knew how—through hard work. And every single one of us who ever stepped foot in that shop has had that same dream.

"You should have the sign on the east wall repainted," I said to my father as I turned away from the pictures to face him. "I think it's about time."

READY TO WEAR

LINDA HANSELL

"Hello, Myrna" my grandmother Bess says to one of her long-time customers as she enters the shop. "A dress came in this week that I think would suit you perfectly. Let me show you." Bess walks her over to a rack of neatly displayed dresses and shows Myrna a belted-at-the-waist printed silk dress in pastel hues.

"Oh, it's beautiful, Bess," coos Myrna. "How much is it?"

"Oh, don't worry about that, Myrna. You can put it on layaway if you want. You know your credit is good here," Bess says, selecting a dress in Myrna's size and handing it to her. "Here. Why don't you go try it on?"

As Myrna makes her way to the dressing room, the door opens again. When the new customer makes her way inside, Bess recognizes the face, but can't immediately come up with her name—a rare occurrence for which Bess will take herself to task later. She quickly ducks behind the counter and surreptitiously opens the slim Salem phone book, scanning each page until she sees the name that matches the face.

"Oh, Mary Jane! So nice to see you," she exclaims, as she makes her way from behind the counter onto the sales floor. "I *have* to show you this Pendleton coat that just came in. It's very stylish...it's what all the girls are wearing these days." She guides Mary Jane down the main aisle toward the coat section in the back of the store.

◆

When my grandparents opened their store on State Street in Salem, Ohio, in 1926, "off-the-rack" clothes were becoming widely available. My grandmother explained that "off the rack" referred to factory-produced clothing sold in standardized sizes, which was replacing the made-to-measure clothing tailored to fit a specific person.

And Hansell's sold the finest "ready-to-wear" women's fashions: dresses, coats, sweaters, blouses, jackets, and blazers, as well as handbags and undergarments such as hosiery and sateen bloomers. The mannequins displayed dresses in the season's newest styles in printed chiffons, printed silks, georgettes, and flat crepes. An advertisement in *The Salem News* in 1930 promoted "frocks with flares," tier skirts, cape and bertha collars, lace collars, jabots, and "dresses in pastel prints and high shades, in any color you may desire."

For many decades after they opened their store, Salem was a thriving town. Hansell's operated alongside department stores such as McCulloch's, Strouss-Hirshberg, JCPenney, and Sears, and discount stores like Woolworths and G.C. Murphy's. Local businesses like Moffet's Men's Wear, Lou Groza Dry Cleaners, Endres & Gross Flowers, Love's Pastries, and Glogan's Hardware provided everything residents needed. Involving three generations of my family, including my Uncle Elliott and my cousin Randy, Hansell's shop thrived for 67 years, making it the longest continually-operating store in Salem.

◆

Salem was founded in 1806 by two Quakers: Zadok Street, a clockmaker from New Jersey, and John Straughan, a potter from Pennsylvania. The name Salem was taken from "Jerusalem," which means "city of peace." Surrounded by Amish farms, the town was a major stop on the Underground Railroad, with at least six houses and a church that provided a safe haven. Salem was also home to the Western Anti-Slavery Society and hosted the third Women's Rights Convention in the United States in 1850, after those in Seneca Falls and Rochester. This progressive spirit faded somewhat during the industrialization of the town, which saw many manufacturing companies, including several tool-and-die manufacturers, open in Salem.

◆

My grandmother took great pride in her role as a professional saleswoman, and she was a master of her trade. Prior to greeting Myrna, my grandmother had examined with her critical eye each dress, skirt, sweater, coat, and blouse hanging on the racks, becoming familiar with the recent arrivals she and my grandfather had purchased on their latest buying trip in New York City. As she leafed through the garments, her experienced fingers read the texture and drape of the fabrics like a blind person's fingers read braille. Her eyes took in color, shape, and style as she committed them to memory.

◆

My memories of the store start from when I was about five or six years old. My family would make the two-hour drive to Salem from our home in the Cleveland suburbs once or twice a year, especially for Thanksgiving. After the holiday meal, my grandparents would take us to the store. Because it was Thanksgiving Day, the store was closed, and we had it to ourselves.

On one hand, I liked going to Hansell's and getting a glimpse of the behind-the-scenes workings of a store. It was fun to wander among the racks and mannequins and run up the stairs in the back to my grandfather's office. On the other hand, it was difficult to fend off my grandmother's exhortations. She was forever trying to interest me in getting a purse (or pocketbook, as she would say.) Having raised three sons, she was thrilled to have a granddaughter to outfit in the stylish garments and accessories from her shop. But I was a bit of a tomboy, and fashion was the furthest thing from my mind. Especially the dowdy, old-people, *supposedly* stylish outfits hanging at my grandparent's store. The clothes at Hansell's store were ready-to-wear, but I was not ready to wear them.

I had more immediate concerns. When I turned six, my brothers had both recently acquired squirt guns. When Grandma Bess asked me what I wanted for my birthday, I told her I wanted my own squirt gun so I could defend myself against my brothers. She was bemused, and not happy.

"Wouldn't you rather have a dress or a pocketbook?" she pressed in her throaty, slightly accented voice. "Here. Come look at these beautiful Rosina pocketbooks. Wouldn't you like to have one?"

I had no interest in, or use for, a pocketbook at that age, and her inability to understand that increased the gulf between us. As a timid child, and one who had had "respect your elders" drilled into her, I didn't know how to tell my grandmother I didn't want a pocketbook. Or a dress. Whether you were family or a customer, it was hard to say "no" to Grandma Bess.

So, my relationship with the store—and with my grandmother—was complicated. Grandma Bess was not a warm and fuzzy grandmother. She didn't hesitate to tell me (or others) what to do, and her bossiness compounded the two-generation gap between us. "You should go to business school after college," she later instructed me, even though she knew my interests lay in the fields of education and psychology.

But some part of me understood that Grandma Bess came from a very different place, both literally and colloquially. She had emigrated with her parents and four siblings from Ukraine to America as a 10-year old girl, landing at Ellis Island on the 4th of July in 1910. Her family made their way to Pittsburgh, where she later met my grandfather, Abraham Hansell.

They married in 1923. Three years later they moved to Salem and opened Hansell's store.

Grandpa Abe was a diminutive, quiet man. I can't remember having any conversations with him, but he seemed kindly. He handled the finances and the paperwork of the store, working six days a week. The extroverted Bess, who had started working retail at age 13 to help her family in Pittsburgh make ends meet, held forth on the sales floor.

◆

"I like it," says Myrna, bringing the dress up to the sales counter. "This silk feels good against my skin. But it's a little too long."

"That's not a problem," Bess replies. "We'll have Gerta hem it for you, and Abe will drop it off at your house tonight." Same-day alterations and delivery were part of my grandparents' commitment to providing the best possible customer service to their clientele.

"You're quite the saleswoman, Bess," Myrna says with a smile and a sigh.

"Aww, go on," Bess replies, with a gurgled laugh.

Grandma Bess writes down Myrna's purchase on a sales slip and rings it up on the 1923 wood McCaskey cash register, the only register used in the store's 67-year history. As she hands the receipt to Myrna, she smiles and says, "Thank you for coming in today, Myrna. I'm sure you'll enjoy wearing this. Now let's go back and have Gerta measure that hem length for you."

◆

By the time I was 14, I was tall enough and had filled out enough to fit into women's clothing. And, as a teenager, on my family's visits to Salem, I would browse the racks of skirts and shelves of Fair Isle sweaters at Hansell's to see what might catch my eye. Later, when I became a full-fledged career woman working in the field of education—while still not a fashion plate—I enjoyed finding a flattering skirt or a nice ensemble to wear to work. By the time my grandmother retired at 89, my closet was home to numerous garments from the store—and even a pocketbook.

The clothes at Hansell's were always ready-to-wear, and I was finally ready to wear them.

THE VILLAGE CARD & GIFT SHOP

SUZANNE SAMUELS

The tiny brass bells tinkled as I opened the door, but my dad was too busy behind the counter to notice. The wooden pegboard above the gift-wrapping table—the one that held the shelves stocked with small gift boxes and bins of hand-made bows—lay in pieces on the floor. In its place, a shiny yellow and black rack with KODAK emblazoned across the top. It was so fancy that for a moment I felt embarrassed for our handmade signs—"STAMPS SOLD HERE!" and "FREE GIFT WRAPPING!"—taped to the wall beside it.

I closed the door. The bells crescendoed. My dad turned towards me.

"Oh, Suzy Q! Hello!" my dad said, looking up. "How was school?"

This same question, every afternoon. If I'd been honest, I would have answered that I hated it. But I just shrugged, mumbled it was okay, and hoped he wouldn't ask any more questions. Thankfully, my dad was so focused on Windexing the Plexiglas front of the Kodak rack that I don't think he heard me at all. After several circuits of spraying, swiping, and inspecting, he stepped back from the rack.

"How do you like it?"

"Uh, it's nice," I stammered, taking in the stack of boxes with strange markings I didn't understand. 100. 200. 400.

"Film," he said. "Our new business."

Just after New Year's, my dad had discovered that a CVS would be opening in a new strip mall down the road. "They got Hallmark," my dad had said quietly when he delivered the news at dinner that night.

"Getting Hallmark" had been our crowning achievement, years ago, when we first opened our card shop on the South Shore of Staten Island. Holding the letter from its Kansas City headquarters in his hands, my dad had decreed that this was a "feather in our cap." "Getting Hallmark" was what set our store apart from other card stores. That five-point gold crown in our window. That slogan: When you care enough to send the very best.

Now CVS would have all of that.

And three times as many square feet.

And parking. A freshly paved asphalt lot with rows and rows of spots. No one there would have to hunt for a space along the street and hope they had a nickel for the meter.

I headed towards the back room to hang up my jacket and book bag. Past the Russell Stover Candy rack, its top two shelves loaded with half-price hearts from Valentine's Day. The still-unclaimed stuffed animals. The blank autograph books and diaries. When I returned to the counter, Dad was dabbing little price stickers onto the side of each roll of film. The pegboard lay on the floor, next to the hammer and a crow bar. I tried not to think of my dad, struggling to remove that board from the wall. The cardiologist had warned that physical exertion might bring on another heart attack. Maybe he wouldn't survive that one. I felt that old familiar ache in my throat. My dad was an invalid. But now, he wasn't grimacing or clutching his chest, like he had before his last attack. No. He was smiling, like he'd created a work of art.

"We'll need to tell our customers." My dad's arm swept grandly towards the rack. "Kodak film. The real deal. We sell and develop film." He was looking wistfully into the distance—at what, I couldn't tell. He tucked the *New York Times* crossword puzzle under his arm and headed towards the back room. In a few minutes, he'd be asleep, head on his chest, arms hanging limply by the sides of the chair. This was happening more and more.

Before he turned to go, he smiled. "It's the wave of the future, Suzy Q. The wave of the future." I tried not to notice how gaunt his face was, or how the deep blue veins crisscrossed his temples. He was a businessman before his heart attack, I reminded myself. He knew what to do. After all, we were still afloat, while the other card store in our town had gone under. *Bankrupt*, I'd heard my dad's mortician friend Tim whisper. *Bankrupt* meant you were forced to sell everything. All the cards. The gift wrap. The stuffed animals. The bisque figurines. *Bankrupt* was a CLOSED sign that no one ever flipped back OPEN. An EVERYTHING FOR SALE sign taped across the front window.

"We sell film now," I said to my first customer, a woman whose cigarette ash was so long that I worried she might set fire to the cards she'd laid on the counter. Two whiny kids clung to her as she tried to wrest her wallet from her handbag. I pushed the Hallmark Gold Crown ashtray closer to her. She flicked the ash onto the floor.

One of the kids spun the rack with the tiny porcelain animal figurines on it; the other pawed at the Russell Stover caramel bars on the counter. My dad had put the candy there as an impulse buy—something he'd read about in *Small Business Daily*, or one of those magazines. Other than my Grandpa, who opened with my dad every morning and ate at least one of those bars before noon, I don't think anyone had been enticed.

I flipped the cards over and started to add up the prices: 35 cents + 25 cents + 35 cents. 95 cents + tax = $1.02. I could do the calculation in my head, though a few customers made me write it on the scratch pad, like a math problem. Or like the store ledger. Before school that morning, I'd gone into the kitchen and found my dad hunched over the ledger, the reds bleeding onto the page. Maybe it was my imagination, but since the CVS had opened last month, there was less and less black. No one had to tell me that red ink wasn't good. Just like no one had to point out that every day, my dad was engaged in a game of Russian Roulette with his unreliable heart.

"We sell film," I said, louder now. The brat spun the rack hard. One of the tiny porcelain lambs went airborne. The woman tossed a buck on the counter and grabbed hold of the kid's hand. A moment later, they were gone.

I had just retrieved the lamb, with its now-broken foreleg, when the next customer approached the counter. A woman about my mother's age, with dark circles under her eyes. It looked like she hadn't brushed her hair in days. Two cards. One sympathy, one blank. Sixty-six cents. She fished around in her bag. After a few moments, she pulled out a credit card. Without thinking, I looked back at the small, handwritten sign near the Kodak display:

Credit Card $15 Dollar Minimum

"I don't know how to run the machine," I said, not looking her in the eye. I liked using the machine: slipping the credit card into the slot, covering it with a carbon copy sales slip and sliding the imprinter over it. But there was the matter of the minimum. The credit card company charged 7 percent for every sale, and Dad said we needed to make enough profit for the transaction to make sense.

I called for my dad. He took one look at the register display with its .66 TOTAL SALE and the woman's credit card on the counter. Without a beat, he lifted the heavy metal credit card machine from its box, placed a sales slip on top, ran the imprinter over it, and wrote *66 cents* onto the bottom line. The customer signed her first name. She seemed to hesitate before adding her last name, as if she wasn't sure what it was. I watched my dad watching her. When she was done, he handed her credit card back to her.

"Have a good day," he said, smiling gently. "Take care." He headed back to his office, and I tried to hide my disappointment in his breaking his own rule.

Finally, my last customer of the day. A cranky old lady who asked me to read sister birthday cards to her. Each and everyone, even the 50 cent cards that we both knew she'd never buy. As I rang up her 15 cent card, I gestured towards the Kodak display.

"We sell film now," I said, sliding the card into a paper bag. "And we develop it, too."

She sneered at me. "What do I need that for?" She grabbed the bag from the counter, her fingers gnarled, like a witch's. "I got nothing I want to remember."

I thought of that sappy Kodak ad on the television. It opened with an old woman standing in front of a house with a SOLD sign on the lawn. As that song, "Remember the Times of Your Life," played in the background, the scene changed. First, that woman was a bride. Then a mother. Then a grandmother.

Those were the kind of customers we needed. The ones Kodak could bring in. People who'd buy lots of film. And 50 cent cards. And the biggest Russell Stover hearts—the ones that cost $14.95.

After the witchy old woman had slammed the front door behind her, my dad came out of the back room.

"How'd we do?" he asked, his eyes scanning the Kodak display, looking for any empty slots. I saw him blink, hard, the only sign that he was disappointed. I wanted to explain: I'd told all of them about the film: the mother with her spoiled brats, the sad woman with her credit card, the mean old lady. None of them were interested.

My dad hitched up his shoulders. "It's alright. It might take a little while. But once people know we have Kodak, they'll come here for their film and photos."

Yes, I thought. With enough of those Kodak grandmothers from TV, our store could stay alive.

◆

Just after St. Patrick's Day—a minor holiday in the card and gift business, meriting only a few rows of cards and a small spinning rack of "Kiss Me I'm Irish" pins and shamrock-beaded necklaces—our film business surged. I came in one afternoon to find that we'd sold four 200s.

My dad was excited. The real money came in developing the film, he'd said, not in the initial sale. For this reason, we'd put foil labels with Village Card and Gift Shop on the bottom of every box of film. As if the film would find its way back to us, like some strange technicolor salmon. On a scratch pad on the counter, my dad had already worked out the profit for the developed film. A buck seventy-five per roll; seven dollars for all four. We couldn't go bankrupt if we were bringing in almost two dollars a roll. With over 100 rolls on our rack, that would mean $200 bucks. If we developed that much film—every month, or maybe even every few weeks—our store would stay afloat.

I thought it would take a week or two for that customer to shoot their four rolls of film. But a few days later, I arrived to find the Kodak bag by the register, with all four rolls of film nestled inside, handwritten receipts rubber-banded around each. I struggled to make out the customer's name: MIKE (Screaming Eagle) JOHNSON, in my dad's familiar handwriting.

"This is a good sign." Holding up the bag, my dad smiled. Yes, I thought. A good sign.

A few days later, the canary-yellow Kodak delivery truck pulled up outside our store, and a khaki-wearing delivery man handed over the developed photos. My dad reverentially tucked these into the expanding file folder marked "AWAITING PICKUP."

I wasn't there when Mike Screaming Eagle picked up his photos or when he dropped off the next batch of canisters to be developed. But Mr. Eagle's business must have confirmed my dad's faith in film. He affixed the Kodak sticker to our front window, next to the signs for Hallmark cards and Russell Stover candies. But except for two or three other sales that month, Mike Screaming Eagle was our only Kodak customer. Most other people seemed to ignore the film developing ads my dad had hung next to the yellow rack, the ones that commanded "READY, AIM, FLASH" and pronounced Kodak *America's Storyteller.*

I was at the counter the day Mike Screaming Eagle came in for his latest batch of photos. He was the tallest person I'd ever seen. He wore a pleather jacket with sleeves that were too short and a tear above the left breast pocket that had been repaired with electrical tape. His fingertips were stained brown; the skin on his face looked dusty, faded. He pulled a small strip of paper from his shirt pocket.

"My film back?" he said, placing the perforated slip on the counter. His voice was cool. When he looked at me, it seemed he wasn't seeing me at all.

There were three envelopes in the "AWAITING PICKUP" folder. Rubber-banded together and labeled *Mike Screaming Eagle.*

"Uh. Mr. Screaming Eagle?" I stammered.

He nodded.

My dad had told me how to ring up photos. Subtract the 50 percent deposit from the total due. Put the money into the Kodak pouch next to the cash register. But Mike Screaming Eagle hadn't paid a deposit. Stranger still was the fact that the TOTAL DUE had been scratched out and a new number penciled in. Instead of owing $10.50—which would have been $3.50 a roll, with Kodak and us splitting the profit—Mr. Eagle owed only $7.50.

I was still puzzling over this when the doorbells jingled and my dad returned from Delco Drugs with a bag tucked under his arm.

"Mike!" My dad's voice was friendly. "Did you see your photos? The lighting seems to be better. The lab said it did the best it could."

Mike Screaming Eagle was pulling photographs from one of the envelopes. He said nothing about my dad looking at the photos first—*was he even allowed to do that?* Instead Mike kept silent, flipping through one pile after another, his brow furrowed.

"So, what do you think?" Dad asked.

Mr. Eagle handed my dad the photos.

Dad leafed through the stack. "Here. This is the one I thought looked particularly good," he said, handing Mike Screaming Eagle a single picture. The others, he placed on the counter. I glanced down at the pile. On top, a picture of Mr. Eagle in full headdress, the feathers like a crown around his head and cascading over his shoulders. The photo seemed off-center, like whoever was looking through the viewfinder didn't know exactly where to point the camera.

"This one's pretty good," my dad said, holding up the photo. Here, Mike Screaming Eagle was looking almost directly at the camera. "You did this yourself?"

Mr. Eagle nodded.

"How do you like it?" My dad's voice was small. Like he was begging or something. I was suddenly so weak in the knees that I had to grasp the edge of the counter to keep myself from crumpling to the floor. I wanted to be strong—no, I needed to be strong—because my dad was so weak. So I did what I could do. I clasped my hands behind my back and prayed for the kind of magic that would make those photos perfect.

Mr. Eagle grunted.

My dad slipped the Kodak ledger from the shelf beneath the register and opened it. Running his finger across the row, he said, "With the discount for re-doing the film, it comes to $5.25. How does $5 sound to you?"

Mike Screaming Eagle threw a five-dollar bill on the counter. Tucking the photos under his cracked pleather-clad arm, he left the store. After he had gone, my dad smoothed out the bill and placed it, almost reverentially, into the Kodak return envelope.

It wasn't my place to ask. But I just kept thinking about the red ink on the ledger. "Dad," I asked, sheepishly. "What about our profit?"

"No profit on reprinting."

I wanted to say that the reprinting was the lab's fault, not ours. If anyone should eat the profit it should have been Kodak. Before I could speak, though, my dad swept his hand to the side, dismissively. "Anyway, he's a good customer. American Indian. The real deal. And it's hard to take a photo of yourself. He really wanted one in that headdress."

I imagined Mr. Eagle alone in his house, trying to snap his own photo. While my dad was here, combing over roll after roll of photos, hoping for the one, good photo. Without a penny to show for it.

I looked around at my store. The tin ceilings with their elaborate patterns, as beautiful to me as the ceilings of the Sistine Chapel. The way the light played on the glass shelves, casting dozens of tiny rainbows of color across the figurines and glassware. The speaker we flicked on just before we opened, and the Muzak, our store's soundtrack. The expectancy that came with every mail delivery. All the "Thank yous" and "Have a good days." If I hadn't seen that ledger, I never would have guessed that my little store was dying.

◆

"Wrap each in pink or yellow foil," Dad had said, pointing to the metallic rolls on the desk. "A bow on top. You know how to make it look nice."

It was two weeks before Mother's Day. I'd been in the back room all week, making bows. Winding the thin, pastel ribbon around the metal arm of the bow-maker, punching the hole and affixing the curling ribbon that held it all in place. When I was finished, I'd return the bow-maker to its place on the wide window sill. Outside, I could see our backyard, and beyond it, to the lumberyard, with its buzz saws and pick-up trucks.

On the floor were fifty hyacinths and tulip plants. The smell was so overpowering that it made me a little sick to my stomach. But Mother's Day. Bigger even than Christmas in the card and gift game. Dad had decided we should sell plants for the big day. He'd found an old flower cart at the dump and spray-painted it white.

As always, he'd done the calculations. If we sold each plant for $2, we'd make a $1 profit. Not counting the cost of the bows, which we usually sold for 35 cents each, or the foil wrapping or ribbons. And not counting the time involved to find and paint the flower cart, or to buy and assemble the plants. All that should figure into the bottom line. But, of course, it hadn't.

After I'd assembled the first six plants, I brought them to the counter. My dad was talking with Dave, a gangly, red-headed man who, despite his 6-foot-3 frame, reminded me of a leprechaun. A loud, creepy leprechaun. Dave came in once or twice a week. I can't remember if he ever bought anything.

"My mother. Uh, my mother. Not feeling good." Dave jerked his head back and forth. Despite the weather, he was wearing a winter parka. He wrung his knit beanie cap between his super-sized hands.

My dad spoke so quietly that I couldn't hear what he was saying. I felt like I was intruding. I cleared my throat. My dad glanced up.

"Dave," he said, gesturing towards the tray of flowers I was holding. "What do you think of our new business venture?"

"Oh. Nice," Dave stammered. "Pretty. Oh. Flowers."

My dad picked up the biggest tulip plant on the tray. "For your mother," he said, handing the pot to Dave.

The blood was rushing in my ears. The whole point of those plants was to make more money. To save our store from bankruptcy. But now my dad was just giving them away. I clenched my fists and dug my fingernails into my palms to keep myself from saying anything.

"She'll like this," my dad said. Dave stood there, his mouth silently opening and closing. Like one of the fish they kept in the tanks at the fish market around the corner. After a moment, he pulled his scrunched-up hat onto his spiky hair. The only movement was the trembling of those tulips in his hands.

After Dave left, I followed my dad outside to the newly painted cart. I had to admit: the flower-covered cart looked good standing there, the black and gold Hallmark sign on the wall behind it. Later, my mother would come and fuss over the cart a bit. But for now, it was just me and my dad. We loaded the plants onto the cart. Bigger tulips on the bottom shelves; hyacinths on top. The pink and yellow foil shimmered in the sunlight.

"We're gonna do well with this," my dad said when we were done. "Cards, candy, flowers. One-stop shopping."

◆

Dad and I were walking from the car into the Acme supermarket when I saw the plant display: Two for $3. Tulips and hyacinths. Even bigger than our flower cart plants. My heart was beating so hard I thought it would explode. I wanted to hide my discovery from my dad, so while he went to get a shopping cart, I stood with my back to the display like a human shield. But of course, he saw.

Maybe it was because of those Acme flowers that Dad decided to open the store on Mother's Day that year. "A smart move," he kept saying in the week leading up to the big day. People would stop by after church or before heading to their brunches or dinners. The truth was that we had so many plants left, and time was ticking. They'd already reached peak bloom. Nobody would want them once their flowers had dropped.

On Mother's Day morning, I'd overheard him talking with my grandfather. He would drop the plants to half price. "Or two for $3," he said. I wondered if he'd been thinking of Acme's sale. But when I got to the store the next day, I saw he hadn't sold even one plant on Mother's Day. The tulip petals were drooping, the hyacinth blooms were brown on their edges. When I put my nose to the clusters, they smelled faintly of decay. A total bust. I started to calculate our loss, then stopped. I just couldn't bear it.

I was there the next day when Tim the Mortician came in. Holding his manicured hand out to my dad, he asked, "How ya doing?" He was younger than my dad, his beard perfectly trimmed, not a hair out of place. Like an Irish Tony Manero from *Saturday Night Fever*. I think I had a crush on him. They chatted and laughed about the new Garfield comic and an ad Tim had seen for an edible chocolate Monopoly set. After a while, Tim buttoned his overcoat and turned to go. My dad pointed at the wilted flowers on the stand.

"Those are the flowers I was telling you about."

Tim nodded. "Nice."

"Think you can use them?"

"Sure. I'll plant them next to the parking lot. Next year, it'll be nice to have some spring color back there."

"Great. I'll bring them to you tomorrow morning."

They shook hands. Tim left the store, the bells gently tinkling behind him.

Then it was on to the next order of business. "Dads and Grads," my father said, pointing toward the front window. It was my job to decorate the window for each holiday.

I took apart the Mother's Day display, unclipping the Hallmark cards that hung on the clotheslines across the window and putting back the milk-glass vases, the sweet figurines of mother and child, and the display boxes of Russell Stover candy.

After I'd put together the window—a mélange of mortarboards, #1 GRAD mugs, and BEST DAD plaques—my dad came outside with me to look at it from the sidewalk.

"This'll bring them in." He smiled, the fading light playing on his gaunt face and neck. "A masterpiece, Suzy Q. As always." Still looking at the display, my dad murmured, "This...this is something CVS doesn't have."

I felt like I was standing on the edge of a cliff, the ground beneath my feet beginning to crumble. Because 15-year-old me could see, even if my father couldn't. It didn't matter if we had a nice window display. Or Hallmark. Or Kodak. We'd never be able to compete. It was a terrible knowledge to have. I wanted to take his hand and gently tell him. He needed to know. But I was terrified he'd collapse on the street, his heart broken beyond repair.

Later, after my dad couldn't navigate without that portable oxygen tank, he tried to sell the store. There were potential buyers, at least at first. But when they considered those ledgers—lined up neatly on the shelf in the back room—I knew they must have seen all that red ink. We'd been barely breaking even, all those years. They understood, even if my dad could not, that the Village Card and Gift Shop, all 2,000 square feet of it, would never be profitable.

We closed quietly. No bankruptcy. No EVERYTHING FOR SALE sign across the window. My dad just turned the OPEN sign to CLOSED one last time.

A short time later, Dad was gone, too. It was at his wake that I got a sense of what he may have meant that June day, as we stood outside looking at the grads and dads window. We did have something that CVS didn't have. It wasn't the cards or gifts, or the candy or the film. The customers came for something they couldn't buy at CVS, or maybe anywhere.

My dad didn't know all their names. But so many of them came to his wake. The little old ladies, who had to press their faces to the guest book to sign their condolences. Mike Screaming Eagle, in a polo shirt and slacks. Dave, fidgeting in the back row. And Tim, gently laying a hand on my dad's casket. While in a bed outside the funeral home, my dad's tulips and hyacinths bloomed.

MY FATHER'S STORE: BUILT TO SUIT

JOAN TAYLOR CEHN

In 1952, when I was two years old, my parents moved to a small town in northern New Jersey. Though it had a train station and was considered a bedroom community of New York City, the population at that time was only around 3,000. This is where my father opened his first store, a men's and boy's clothing store on Main Street when Main Street WAS the main street. My father chose this town, I later learned, because there was no competition, no other men's stores in town.

Starting at about age six, when school let out each day, I walked the four blocks, by myself, to my father's store on Main Street. I learned the landmarks along the way. The train station at one end of the street followed by the five-and-dime, the dairy store where we bought our milk and ice cream, the luncheonette counters with their rows of revolving stools where you could get a tuna sandwich and a milkshake. Then came the ladies' dress shop, the jewelers, and, finally, Hank Taylor's Ramsey Men's Shop, my father's store.

Farther down Main Street was the grocery store, the only one in town. Next, the Ramsey Cinema, which caused quite a bit of excitement when it opened and soon became a meeting place for kids, especially for Saturday matinees. At one of these matinees, I screamed along with all the other kids through a showing of the hair-raising *Journey to the Center of The Earth*, one of the first movies I remember seeing.

I was always happy to arrive and see my father in his store; it was a constant. It felt like security and it was. I was safe in the knowledge that my father would always be there. I don't recall ever being scared to walk the distance by myself. Perhaps because it seemed like all the store owners on Main Street knew me. This had its upside when I was young, but a certain downside later. In high school I once flirted with the idea of buying cigarettes to help shed my "good girl" image. The hope was soon extinguished by the realization that I would never get away with it, as I was certain the purchase would be followed up with a phone call from the store owner tattling my indiscretion to my father. If it takes a village to raise a child, then Main Street was that village for my family and me.

Growing up, I spent many afternoons at Ramsey Men's Shop, watching the customers come and go. My father knew most of them by name and those he didn't, he would make it his business to know. He'd ask after family members and, usually, tell a joke or share an interesting anecdote. People left laughing or smiling. My father believed deeply in the notion that "the customer is always right." My father was easy to talk to and made everyone feel comfortable. I knew this was a skill of his, and I paid attention.

When I was young, he would put me to work breaking down the cardboard boxes the merchandise arrived in. But when I got older he put me "on the floor" where I asked customers how I could assist them. I learned how to select a tie to match a shirt, and how to suggest, perhaps, a nice vest to go with that shirt.

A sales counter in the back held my father's monogrammed boxes and specialty wrapping paper. Fascinated, I would observe my father cutting the paper to the exact size needed and neatly covering the box, securing it with Scotch tape. He took pride in the preciseness of that task, which soon became a favorite task of mine. Customers left the store with beautifully wrapped packages in my father's signature look.

I was also fascinated by the elaborate metal cash register that sat prominently on the side counter. Its ornate numbered keys, when punched, made a ringing sound and forced the money drawer at the bottom to pop out. It wasn't until high school that I was allowed to operate that register. My father watched with a careful eye as I did the math to calculate the change due; he'd taught me how to do that while slowly counting back the bills directly into the customer's hand.

I was not the only one who got into the act. My older brother was recruited to sell as well—and he had the envious advantage of being able to wear the beautiful clothes with their rich fabrics (no polyester or synthetics) that my father sold, which certainly added to his salesmanship and success. My mother, with her head for numbers, oversaw the buying, inventory, and accounting. After discovering how much the local tailor charged to alter and cuff pants, she learned how to do that too, using her old Singer sewing machine, and then added that to her job description.

Though my broad-shouldered father played football for Michigan State, he took great pride in his elegant hand-lettered signs. I would watch as he used a pencil and straightedge to draw parallel lines between which he crafted his beautiful letters into words. ALL SHIRTS 20% OFF or BUY TWO TIES, GET ONE FREE. Black and red markers were his tools, and the signs the product of his artistic side.

One of my father's favorite activities was "dressing the window." Today it would be called something like "visual merchandising." Not ever really knowing what might catch a customer's eye, my father followed the "more is better" approach and filled the small window with as many items as would fit. This was especially evident in his Christmas window display. He'd place two rather large male mannequins in the center of the window, attired smartly in slacks, mohair, or cashmere sweaters, and sporty ski jackets. Their outfits would be completed with brightly colored wool hats, leather gloves, and warm scarves, as if they were about to set out for a brisk walk in the snow.

My father would elaborately tie red and green ribbons around endless stacks of folded shirts, sweaters, socks, and neckties and place them around the window filling in any empty spaces. Finally, he would remove the fragile, slightly dusty Santa from his box in the back room and carefully position it prominently in the window amid a sprinkling of strategically placed fake snow. Across the top of the window he would hang the string of small twinkling red and green lights which illuminated his handmade Merry Christmas sign that was prominently Scotch-taped to the glass.

We entered each Christmas season with great anticipation. The holiday season was an enormously important time for our small family business; we relied on it for our survival. While friends were on vacation, we were in the store selling scarves, gloves, sweaters—anything else not nailed down. We would expectantly await the same few customers who came in year after year right before closing on often frigid and snowy Christmas Eves—after calling first, pleading for us to wait for them. We were always relieved when these loyal customers arrived as we knew their purchases would be significant, usually hundreds of dollars' worth of gifts. And these last-minute shoppers were relieved and grateful as well that we were there.

Hank Taylor's was always there for its community. Many decades later, at my 40th high school reunion, male classmates shared memories of coming into the store and buying their Scout uniforms as young boys, later on, their varsity sweaters, and later still, their sport jackets for their first job interviews.

In the late 1960s, a developer arrived in Ramsey and revealed plans to build a "shopping center" on the edge of town. My father was offered a space in this new strip mall. Much discussion ensued between my parents about leaving downtown. They concluded it was best to stay. Neither could see the evolution that was taking place in small-town America. To them the demise of Main Street was unimaginable.

RAISE/RAZE

KIMBERLY ENCE

The old slaughterhouse sits idle, eighteen paces from the banks of the Snake River. I'm certain of the distance because I measured it the other day, beginning with my heels at the loading docks of the building, stretching my legs in a purposeful march, and planting my feet eighteen times before I stood at the water's edge.

Counting is part of remembering.

As a child, the distance between the building and the river seemed much farther. My siblings and I talk regularly about tearing the building down, but we just can't bring ourselves to do it.

"I feel sentimental about it," I said during last month's board meeting.

"Same," said my brother.

Our eldest sibling spins his pen on the table, neither agreeing or disagreeing. He's almost sixty, old enough to think about retirement. We all know that it's a valuable piece of riverfront property, especially if the dilapidated building were gone.

"We'll talk about it next month," our youngest sister says, moving her finger down the agenda to the next item of business.

None of us objects.

Our father is missing from this meeting, not because he's eighty years old and slowing down, but because he's eighty years old and ramping up. He's got more pressing, profitable business meetings to attend. It's okay that he's absent. The four of us don't want to discuss razing the building because he would, without a doubt, suggest a repurposing of the structure and its antiquated equipment. Most likely we would find ourselves *not* retiring but wading elbow deep into the dog food industry, or learning the artisanal sausage business, or brewing vats of bait for Siberian bear hunters (all of these ideas he's mentioned at one time or another). Dad is all about reinvention and reinvigoration, not retirement and demolition. More than any of us, he's emotionally attached to the brick and mortar of our past. More than any of us, he's counting precious years and dollars and memories.

When Mom and Dad purchased the slaughterhouse in 1967, the transaction was a BOGO—buy a business, and the house next door was thrown in for free. Neither structure was much to look at. The exterior of the four bedroom/two bath house was covered in rough-hewn, clapboard siding, chocolate brown with a brick chimney. Cat face spiders loitered in the corners. The slaughterhouse was a squat cinderblock building painted seafoam green and peeling from years of neglect. Fresh out of graduate school, the *buy-one-get-one* was Dad's first business and Mom's first house. But separating the two in that way, business and home, would be misleading. To our young family they were practically one and the same.

Our business and house were tightly hemmed in by the river to the west, McCarty's junkyard, ten paces to the north, and the Yellowstone Highway, a stone's throw to the east. The highway and the railroad tracks that ran parallel through our small town of Idaho Falls were dotted for miles with industrial businesses that catered to the moving parts of town. Gas stations, the stockyard, a trucker's cafe, and second-rate motels clung to the economy that traveled north toward Yellowstone National Park and south toward Utah.

Of course, fifty years and a sprawling community have changed my old neighborhood. Mom's clapboard house was demolished long ago. A Candlewood Hotel & Suites stands where the junkyard used to be. City landscapers have removed the willows, weeds, and purple thistle that used to grow thick along the banks of the river. Manicured grass now meets the water's edge and a walking path meanders for miles upstream from the hotel. Some of the original slaughterhouse foundation and walls are still there, but we have not killed livestock there since the late-70s when making beef jerky became more lucrative than processing pork chops and rump roasts.

We've been in the beef jerky business for fifty years. The building is now an architectural modge-podge reflecting decades of growth and modification. Like rings in the trunk of a tree, I can trace my life in this place. I recognize concrete foundations that represent my pre-K years, cinder block walls from when I was eleven, machines I knew as a teenager, and warehouses built after I went to college.

I count eight paces from the corner of the jerky plant to the back door of the hotel.

The buildings are too close.

A beef jerky factory and a hotel make for awkward neighbors. Up until a year ago, when we mothballed the building, the hotel was giving refunds to guests because visitors didn't appreciate the smell of beef jerky wafting from the smokehouse chimneys, past the hotel porte-cochére, through the sliding glass doors and into the lobby.

Beef jerky roasting in the smokehouse smells like nighttime and summer and my father working. The smell takes me back to when my feet were small, probably a size four. The smokehouse doors of the plant are wide open, making the concrete floor warm underneath my bare toes. Hot air pours into the room and steams up the windows. My feet are relatively clean because I've just taken a bath, put on my pajamas, and run barefoot to the jerky plant to check on him. If Dad finishes pulling racks of beef jerky from the smokehouse by 9:30, we might make it to the local A&W drive-in before it closes at 10.

"I could sure use a root beer float," he says to me.

Sweat runs down his forehead, neck, arms, and drips from his elbows. I grab a piece of jerky from one of the metal screens and hold it tight in my fist while I gnaw and suck warm, smoky juice from the end of the stick. Beef fibers fray and expand in my mouth. I bite off the soggy end, chew, swallow, and start all over again while I run a hundred strides back home in the twilight. Pebbles from the asphalt wedge between my toes. The cool, summer air makes me shiver while the stick of meat between my salty lips hardens like an old cigar.

"Sh-tart the car, Mom," I yell into the dark, my teeth still clenched around the stump. "He'sh almoshh done."

Just before the BOGO of 1967, Dad was a meat science Ph.D. candidate at the University of Illinois. I was an infant. My brothers were six and four. Our grandmother called from Idaho to tell Dad that there was a meat packing business for sale. He flew to Idaho Falls. He remembers "a dirty little old beast of a plant, about as poor as I had ever seen." But he was excited about the opportunity to buy his own business. Still, feeling uncertain about the decision, he brought photos back to Illinois and showed images of the slaughterhouse to his graduate advisor, Dr. Breidenstein. The professor laughed and tossed the photos onto his desk. "I cannot believe you would even consider doing such a thing," he said. "That place is a rat trap. You'll spend the rest of your life with shit under your fingernails and blood to your elbows. With your education, you can do so much better."

Apparently, that was neither the reaction nor the advice my father wanted to hear. As he tells me this story, decades later, the memory irritates him all over again, "Breidenstein didn't have any idea what motivated me and where I had come from." My young father gathered the photos from his professor's desk and quit school. Mom and Dad loaded our belongings into a station wagon and we moved to Idaho.

To be truthful, Dad's decision to leave his Ph.D. program was probably less about Breidenstien's reaction and more about the fiscal realities of a restless twenty-something with three young children and a wife to feed. While in school, Dad washed dishes at a frat house and raised a small herd of pigs. He also concocted a recipe for beef jerky. He produced it in the animal science lab in his department and sold it to his friends on campus.

With the move to Idaho, he forgot about beef jerky and focused on making the meat packing business a success. He slaughtered the livestock of local farmers and ranchers, wrapping their meat for custom sale. He supplied restaurants and grocery stores with ground hamburger meat. He cranked out enough hot dogs for the county fair, Boy Scout camps, and rodeos, but hamburgers and hot dogs weren't enough to pay the bills. Dad swam in debt. Bankruptcy threatened to drown him. He recalled, "One day the banker from the SBA came to the plant and told me they were shutting the doors to retain what was left of our business. I told him to go away. I wasn't quitting."

According to the bankers, our meat packing business could survive for about four more months. Dad hadn't made jerky since leaving college, but he had an old smokehouse in the plant and plenty of meat, so he secured a loan from a different bank and named his new venture "King B Jerky."

He sold the beef sticks to pubs, bars, and convenience stores along the I-15 corridor. Every other jerky product on the shelf was dry, tough to chew, and sold for 15 cents. Our King B Jerky was labor intensive: hand cut from flank steak, mixed and marinated with secret spices, manually sorted onto screens and pulled from the smokehouses one heavy rack at a time. Retail price for King B Jerky was 25 cents. Consumers didn't blink at the price; they gobbled up every stick that he placed on the shelf. King B Jerky helped to pay the bills. The SBA backed off.

In some of my first memories of Dad, he's dressed in black rubber boots, a hard hat, and a white lab coat spattered with blood. I wasn't alarmed by his appearance. Those were his work clothes. Kids from the other side of the highway and railroad tracks thought he was frightening, but they often invited themselves over after school so they could watch him work.

There was a window screen where we could stand outside the kill floor and watch my father slaughter cows and pigs. With their eyes wide, saliva thick in their throats, ears ringing with gunshots and screaming pigs, the kids were transfixed by the machinations of a kill floor. As a restless grade-schooler, I tired quickly of the horse flies and mosquitoes that gathered with us at the screen. As far as I was concerned, every show was a rerun and the stinging insects made for a miserable matinee. My friends usually lingered, not quite making a connection between the drama playing out in front of them and the pork chops they would eat for dinner.

I didn't notice the subtle shift from bankruptcy to break-even. To a child it all looked the same: We still ate meat and potatoes, we still shopped at the thrift store, and we always worked. For me, punching a time clock after school had little to do with a paycheck. Work was also my play, my imaginary world, my social life, and my pocket-full of street smarts.

My first job in the slaughterhouse was managing the soda machine. It sat just outside of the office door, close to the break room and the loading docks. My arms were scrawny. They could not carry a whole crate of glass soda pop bottles so I portaged them, two bottles at a time, from the storage closet to the blue Pepsi machine. I wrestled with the heavy door. The metallic air inside was chilled by whining fan belts and 1970s fluorocarbons.

It wasn't the cool air that gave me gooseflesh, nor was it the mountains of quarters, dimes, and nickels filling the coin receptacle. It was the *sound* of the machine swallowing money at breaktime, or lunchtime, or at the end of a long, thirsty day. It was the *sound* of coins clinking and tumbling down the machine's parched throat and finally landing with a thud in its belly. With the door open and the machine laid bare I could not only hear the mechanics of the swallowed coin, I could watch the levers, chutes, pulleys, and hinges deliver a coin and make ready a beverage. The colorful lineup of bottle caps, the sound of glass rolling down the metal ramp, the hissing of opened soda—the whole process was an ice-cold symphony of organization, logistics, efficiency, and color-coding. Filling that machine with rainbows of colored syrup didn't seem like work to me. The machine was a life-size toy that doubled as a lubricant in the working system of the plant. Thirsty men and women, essential to our business, expected the pop machine to be filled with cold refreshment. It was my job to keep the team hydrated.

I was promoted from the soda machine as soon as I was tall enough to staple cardboard shipping boxes. The awkward machine that I worked with was just over 50" tall, only a few inches wide, and had a lever at the bottom; stepping on the lever activated the staple mechanism on the top. The stapler stood rigid in the attic of the plant. I spent hours in the attic, a magical, musty room that I considered my own. My imagination came alive in this space. The narrow staple machine became a skinny, long-necked stork with one foot extended tentatively toward me. I folded the bottom of a cardboard box, slipped it into the bird's blunted beak, and stomped crisply on his extended foot. Wincing in pain, the animal snapped its beak closed, spitting a shiny brass staple into the bottom seam of the box. I stacked the finished boxes to the ceiling, filling the room with skyscrapers of neatly stapled boxes. I imagined the attic as a city, and the bird my cranky friend.

With every birthday it seemed my jobs got dirtier and less inspiring. Cleaning the bathrooms after dozens of employees went home for the day was the worst assignment I ever had, and in a slaughterhouse, there's no shortage of unsavory tasks.

A close second to cleaning toilets was working in the returns department. Actually, for one whole summer, I *was* the returns department. Sticks of moldy beef jerky covered in grayish, greenish fuzz piled up in the warehouse. Because our product was so moist, it molded quickly and customers returned it by the box load. To be written off at tax time, the sticks had to be counted. For three hot, sticky months I counted moldy returns while fragrant spores floated through the air and stuck to my skin.

Dirty jobs I didn't mind so much included dumping and wiping ashtrays, washing chili pepper-red lipstick from coffee mugs, and sweeping lunch remains off the floor of the employee break room. Sometimes I put on the black rubber boots, hairnet, and waterproof apron required in the production areas of the plant so that I could screen jerky; this meant sorting raw, cold strips of meat onto metal screens. My fingers became red and chapped from the spices.

I was too young to be helpful in the office, but Winnie sometimes let me staple or stamp. Her space was filled with the non-violent implements and soft edges of the business: ink pads, tape dispensers, mimeographs, typewriters, telephones with blinking lights, and cigarettes smoldering in ashtrays. Winnie kept a first aid kit in her desk drawer. Even if I scraped my knee at home, I would run over to Winnie's office for a Band-Aid.

My two older brothers had an enviable job. They cleaned the kill floor after closing time. It had high ceilings with chains and hooks dangling to the floor. They used fire hoses to blast every surface with scalding hot water. For a kid it was like bringing a fire hose into the house. The steamy air was heavy with organic matter that you couldn't see but you could smell and taste. When the job was done, the concrete floors were slick and looked like a lake. No more squealing pigs, gutted cows, and ornery men, just metal tables and rows of sharp knives dripping with clean water. Sometimes I was allowed to use the rubber squeegee on a long pole and push water across the floor toward the drain. I can still feel the black rubber boots, a few sizes too big, slipping across an invisible coating of animal fat and hot water.

It was early morning, still dark, when flames devoured the plant. While the four of us kids slept, fire gutted the slaughterhouse and our parents lived the nightmare of it. They ran in and out of the freezers, trying to save the inventory, emerging from the smoke-filled doorways with armfuls of pot roasts and hot dogs. Boxes of beef jerky littered the asphalt parking lot. On his final trip into the flames, Dad grabbed the invoices from Winnie's desk. The paperwork was a record of debts owed to him, a lifeline to the future.

My exhausted mother most likely stood in the dark between the fire and the house, lights and sirens rattling through the tops of her leafless cottonwood trees, over the grass, and across her face. She wondered how to wake us, how to tell us. I don't remember how she woke me or if I smelled the fire on her clothes. I don't remember breakfast that morning. I was only about seven, too young to understand what it all meant. I don't remember my parents worrying, arguing, or crying about the fire.

Curious about my lack of memories that morning some fifty years ago, I called my mother.

"Why don't I remember *you* that morning? Certainly, I would have remembered you crying or frantic with worry?" I asked.

"Probably because I wasn't worried. I knew your dad would take care of us," she replied with a matter-of-factness that I recognize, but not sure that I trust. At seventy-seven years old, she readily admits that she lived every day of their married lives fearful that Dad would lose everything they had worked for because of his next *big idea.* At eighty, he remains fearless. Mom had faith in him all those years ago because, on that morning, she had nothing left to lose.

The outstanding mortgage on the burnt-out building gobbled up all of their insurance money. Without enough funds to rebuild, Dad moved the jerky production to a small plant in Salmon, Idaho. Dad commuted three hours back and forth, several times each week. Despite the fire, our family and business adjusted to the new, upended reality. But there was no pop machine, no stapling stork, no lipstick on coffee cups, and no Winnie to keep me company. I remember feeling lonely as a child. The burnt-out building and vanished employees must have contributed to my isolation.

Tired of being separated from Dad, we decided to spend the summer of 1976 with him in Salmon. My mom, dad, sister, and I lived in a 24-foot trailer. Dad parked our aluminum home in the middle of a horse pasture, next to the Salmon, Idaho jerky plant. My two brothers camped out in a nearby tack shed filled with machinery and mice. It felt like a Laura Ingalls Wilder summer. I swam in the creek, chased frogs, fished, and lived a barefoot life. I received a horse for my birthday. She was a brown and white paint, stubborn, crafty, and slow: perfect for a nine-year-old girl. I spent a week trying to make friends with the horse. I was in the pasture with a bucket of oats when I heard my mom calling. She sounded distressed, so I dropped the bucket and ran to her.

"Get in the car!" she yelled, "Where is your sister? We have to get home!"

The Teton Dam had crumbled and burst that morning, June 5, 1976. A fifteen-foot wall of water swept away entire towns, farms, and 13,000 head of livestock along the Teton and Snake River Valleys. The flood's headwaters wouldn't reach our home in Idaho Falls until early the next morning, so we rushed home from Salmon to try and save our house, or our photos, or whatever we might find when we arrived. In the coming hours, the Snake River swelled beyond its banks.

Towers of sandbags saved our house, but floodwaters crawled up the walls of our burnt-out jerky plant. My brothers converted a large meat tub into a boat. We paddled with 2x4s on floodwaters that had devastated upstream families. We paddled on their tragedy, through our own black skeleton of roofless office space, to the roofless freezers, and through a portal where the front door used to be. The concrete kill floor was an indoor swimming pool filled with murky water.

Beyond the sandbags we watched trees, fences, cars, dead cows, pigs, sheep, and horses rush by, teats-up, in the swollen and muddy river. There was nothing more we could do but watch the grisly parade. I saw, heard, tasted, and smelled the flood—the frightening river, the warm June breeze, the putrid water and the sludge it left behind. More than anything I remember the aftermath: railroad tracks twisted like Slinky toys, houses invaded by topsoil that, for centuries, had nurtured farmers' crops. That same topsoil now carpeted their kitchen floors and filled their old Cadillacs.

Fire and flood punctuated my middle childhood. This is a time when kids develop the ability to see beyond themselves, distinguish between fair and unfair, right and wrong. They can understand feeling two emotions at the same time. They learn empathy and compassion. They turn from fantasy-based games to activities that emphasize winning and losing. I may have been isolated, living on a patch of industrial dirt, but the entire world floated by me that day. Other people's lives floated by me. I knew nothing of the 1970s economic recession, the oil embargo, Vietnam, industrial advancements, or civil rights, but the fire taught me loss. The flood taught me that other people suffer. None of it was fair.

After the waters receded, it felt like the world was covered in impossible mud. I remember trying to heave a shovel-full of the sludge from someone's carport and being surprised at how heavy it was. Strangely enough, if I point to a time in my childhood when my loneliness seemed to lift, it was in those months after our muddy baptism. The time between the flood and the rebuilding of our family business was probably a year, but it felt like an instant, as if the floodwaters washed away the charred building and a new jerky plant suddenly sprang up in the concrete footprint of the original.

Making jerky in the new plant still required hand-intensive labor, but our business was now a modern production facility with advanced machines that could vacuum pack, seal, *and* label bags of jerky. Working in the assembly lines of the new machines required fast hands and laser focus, but not much imagination. My days of stapling storks and carbonated goosebumps were over. Work became something I did for money, not for fun.

Mom, with a decade of riverfront tumult under her belt, was ready for some distance between the places we called home and work. She bought a house at a public auction. It was only five blocks east of the BOGO house and new jerky plant, but it felt much farther than that. Even as a ten-year-old, I knew that the move from one side of the highway to another wasn't just a physical relocation, the distance was social and economic as well.

With my first skateboard underfoot, I explored the smooth sidewalks of town and finally enjoyed a neighborhood full of friends. After four years of early-morning bus rides, I walked to the fifth grade at a reasonable hour. I was on the student council. I won the sixth grade penmanship contest. Our street was named Maple.

Today, on eBay, a vintage King B Jerky snap-back 1980s trucker hat will cost you $44.95. Back in 1980, I commandeered several of those hats from my brother's closet and sold them to my friends at school for $5 each. I don't know what got into me, stealing hats and thinking that nobody would notice. I blame it on the intense, entrepreneurial vibe in our home. Those King B hats were popular among my friends because Dad had just created a buzz in the meat snacks industry with a new product called Jerky Stuff. Teenagers were going crazy for the fluffy, shredded beef jerky in a plastic chewing-tobacco-like can. It fit in the back pocket of their Hash Jeans and made them look badass without rotting their teeth or upsetting their parents.

Jerky Stuff was a practical solution for the pieces of meat leftover during the cutting process. Dad figured that there *must* be a use for the pounds and pounds of wasted meat, but shredding pieces of tough, dried beef into a fluffy substance is tricky. 1980's blenders are not the pulsating, triturating monsters that we know today. Back then, Dad burned the engines out of several blenders before he snuck into Mom's kitchen and stole away with her new Bosch food processor. For this stunt he received several days of Mom's silent treatment. As a kid, I thought her punishment was unfair; he *needed* that equipment for his brilliant plan! As an adult, a mother, and owner in a family business, I understand Mom's fear of losing not only a blender, but everything. As long as home and work remained inseparable to our parents, our childhood home, *her home*, was always vulnerable to his entrepreneurial whims. Mom may have moved us blocks away from the fires and floods, but the most immediate threat (and promise) to our financial security slept beside her every night.

In the end, the tenacity of a German blender combined with American ingenuity created a product that rocked not only the snack industry, but the tobacco industry as well. A tobacco company offered Dad $3 million for the Jerky Stuff business. He refused to sell, so the spurned tobacconist enlisted help from his powerful friends. The tobacco lobby in Washington, D.C., sent King B a nasty, threatening letter. But Dad would not back down. In response, he added a short quip to the Jerky Stuff label: "The product found in this container is a healthy substitute for the cancer-causing chemicals in tobacco."

Jerky Stuff was not the only 1980s idea incubated and hatched in the warmth of Dad's pillow. He was in the bubblegum business, he raised bison, created a skin care line, built a water park and a hotel, started a trucking company, bought a hunting lodge, launched an MLM (Melaleuca, Inc.), and he manufactured fish eggs, plastics, and ice cubes.

Several years ago, we built a new, 200,000-square-foot jerky plant just down river from the original.

Last year, he bought a gold mine.

A few weeks ago, my sister tracked down the keys to the old jerky plant and slipped them into my purse. Before we tear it down, *if* we tear it down, I need to count steps. I need to remember.

"When you're finished, just leave the keys on my front porch, behind the flowerpot," she says. Then she adds, "It's pretty creepy in the old building. I wouldn't go alone."

She's right. Spooky is not just the moldy smell, naked light bulbs buzzing over silent machinery, or the feeling that workers walked away mid-sentence, dropping their rubber boots and hairnets as they left the building—it's the ghosts of people still there. It is the echoes of Winnie's typewriter and chattering, breakroom *abuelas*, the smell of onion salt and paprika in an empty spice room, and a cold smokehouse that, once upon a time, was stoked by an eternal, applewood fire.

I hear the familiar hum of a walk-in freezer. Someone left it running. Inside the freezer is a huge tub on wooden pallets. Were I a ditzy teenager in a horror movie, here's where I'd find a dead body. I hesitate for a moment, then pull back the plastic tarp. Rather than a corpse, I discover a half-ton of frozen meat scraps that Dad has collected off the production floor *just in case* we want to make dog food or grizzly bear bait.

"We gotta tear this place down," I mumble under a frosty breath.

The city of Idaho Falls will not mourn its demolition. The hotel next door will be glad to see us go. The jerky plant was never a cultural anchor like a local hardware store, grocery market, or drug store might be. In the early days of boats and freight cars, it may have been an important stop along the river or the railway, but not anymore.

So, what *will* be lost if we raze the building? Nothing tangible, for sure. Developers will clean up the riverfront and plant grass. Old people will shuffle past on the walking path and say to their grandkids, "I remember when this hotel was a junkyard, and oh yes, on that spot over there," pointing with a shaky, crooked finger, "that was a slaughterhouse."

"What's a slaughterhouse, Grandpa?"

"It's where they kill cows and make hot dogs," he'll say.

The children will be conflicted because they love cows *and* hot dogs.

And then he'll shuffle away, much like my own father walks nowadays. Dad has recently, and inexplicably, lost all of his fingernails and toenails. Although his daily routine would be less painful if he didn't put on his boots and shuffle off to the office or the ranch, he chooses pain because he wants to work.

In his pocket Dad carries a gold coin the size of a thick cucumber slice. I don't know why my brain connects the two, his vulnerable, naked fingers and the gold coin, but they seem relevant to an old man's body and a young man's ambition. Of this I am certain: My father does not equate gold with wealth, rather, it is a measure of his grit. Everytime he reaches into his pocket and feels the weight of that coin, he's probably reminded that a young man, the same one who survived fires and floods, is still with him. The two of them have work to do.

When I walked through the jerky plant a few weeks ago, I looked for something that might fit inside *my* pocket. If I could find a meaningful token to carry around for a few weeks, I might be able to transfer my attachment from a large building to a small, significant object. In the attic, where the stork and I used to staple boxes, I found an amber bottle with a glass stopper. It was old and dusty enough, but irrelevant to my past. I brought the bottle home anyway, hopeful that it might spark a memory. I placed it on my desk. It has failed to inspire or motivate me. What I need is a bottle cap, a brass staple, or an abandoned tube of chili-red lipstick.

I also need a match.

Rather than a wrecking ball or bulldozer, I prefer a Viking's farewell for the old building. Fire is familiar to me. I can imagine the detonation, the inferno, and the furious energy of a fire. The smokehouses will come alive one last time, emitting the smell of applewood smoke and burnt spice. Eventually, firemen in red trucks will roll up and they'll flood the smouldering corpse with water. Charred cinder blocks and impossible mud will remain, but this time there will be no resurrection, just the stapling stork spreading his wings and flapping eight strokes, maybe nine, as he glides above the surface of the Snake River. He'll dip his wing at the bank of the distant shore and head upstream.

"Root beer floats are on me," I'll say to my father as we move toward his pickup truck, and he will agree.

LOOKING SOUTH ON MAIN

NINA GABY

> *"The myth of rural virtue is 50 percent memory. 40 percent hope. And 10 percent marginal living."*
> *– Political scientist Frank Bryan, keynote speech to the Randolph, Vermont Chamber of Commerce, 2001.*

There has been talk of poison down the road. Bushes turned brown, a dog dead. The bizarre death of the woman rumored to be responsible for killing the bushes and the dog. She slipped off her stone wall, was caught under her riding lawn mower, and found several days later. The police asked around, "Did anyone have anything against her?" Apparently no one said anything, but under our breaths we couldn't help but whisper "karma" in remembrance of that sweet Border Collie. Again, this is hearsay, as I suppose is the case with much of the history in small towns such as this.

The village is falling apart. I take care not to lean on the rickety railing of The Fork Shop, the old 1820s pitchfork factory built over the spillway as I toss lint from my pocket to commemorate the New Year. In Jewish tradition we empty our pockets over running water, the custom known as Tashlich, during the days of wonder and awe between Rosh Hashanah, the New Year, and Yom Kippur, the Day of Atonement. We shall cast away our sins, watch them drift downstream. Many of the sins listed relate to voicing scorn towards our neighbors, and I feel I should have more than lint for this somber task.

On Tripadvisor people leave reviews like, "small town USA with a Rockwell vibe," and that our bridge is "history you can walk on," although this is not going to just be the story about how we bought an old inn and lost an old inn on a six mile dirt road in central Vermont.

No longer steady are the rock foundations of the long gone gravure, creamery, blacksmith, and foundry over which the once hard-working stream rushes past, much as it did when the water powered those thriving local businesses. Today, I'm alone with the dog, scraping for crumbs in my pocket, worried about falling the twenty feet into the basin that runs under the shop, where the sluice wheel once spun. I find only the lint and wonder what that means for the year ahead.

Across the main road from the lawn mower accident, Laurence died in the small house, its foundation propped by cinder blocks, the house that had belonged to his mother and his younger, now dead, stepfather Roland. Roland had done odd jobs around the village since long before our time. He was the cross-country trail groomer dragging an old twin mattress frame behind a barely functional snowmobile. He was the short order cook when The Fork Shop was a restaurant, a dishwasher at Green Trails Inn, and finally the garbage pick-up person for most of the twenty homes that lined our main drag.

Roland was what we called a "character," as round as he was tall with a shock of unwashed curly hair that never thinned even when he became so ill. Gruff and unsmiling, though we would have expected joviality from one so round and curly. I suspected it was a marriage of convenience more than one of passion for Roland and the gentle Estelle, and while I don't want to think too much about it, I do hope they found some deeper satisfaction.

We didn't know that Laurence had died. He was the type of guy you'd call an old Vermonter, for whom people would throw in the adjectives "decent" and "quiet," maybe "spare," maybe mention his steady gaze. He'd retired from his foundry job a couple towns over and took on the garbage route from Roland. But then one day Pete came to get the garbage instead. Never said a word about Laurence, leaving us stunned because it's a tiny village and what does it mean when you don't even get the important news? Not even the now-ancient Estelle, in a nursing home, knows that her eldest son has died. Estelle, who is credited with unwittingly introducing Japanese Knotweed into the village because she thought it pretty, exotic like bamboo, never suspecting how it would invade and choke us out.

And since one side of the town doesn't talk much to the other side of the town, there's a natural divide that goes beyond "the famous floating bridge," a tourist attraction in days gone by, when even a simple wooden bridge spanning a 300-foot lake was cause for an outing. Nowadays, fewer people stop to ask if they can really drive over it. "Yup," I say when they do. "It's a state highway."

I haven't spoken to my neighbor in the south since the Yom Kippur woodpile incident of 2009. My old best friend to the north and I stopped talking when I complained about her husband shoving me—like I was supposed to not say anything even though everyone saw it happen? In retrospect, should I have let it go and not thought suspiciously about our own row of slender pines suddenly turning brown? Is that how people survive? "Yes," I would say to my younger self from the unsteady vantage point of today. "Yes."

And now Laurence's younger brother James is dying of brain cancer in that same house, with its foundation of cinderblocks. People say he's without electricity and the pipe from the spring on the dead lawnmower lady's property is broken, so there's no fresh water flowing under the road. People might say he's "proud" but I'm still afraid to go down there, even though I think about making up the chicken pie casserole his mother taught me back as a new innkeeper, that authentic Vermont dish that my guests loved so, even though I added petite green peas to add a pop of color. I'm afraid of the memory of Laurence's younger and once robust brother ambling up and down the main road of the village with a machine gun strapped across his chest, giving me the evil eye for a certain right-of-way snafu. Oh come on, I want to say, there are always right-of-way snafus in places like this. Look at Randy, Paula, Kenny, and Pam. There were days we couldn't let our kid out because of all the shooting going on in Kenny's backyard. And even though Chip, the lawnmower lady's neighbor, told me that Laurence's brother gave away his guns, the thought of brain cancer and the possibility of firearms doesn't sit too well. So no chicken pie.

Maybe it's our own little cancer cluster down there. Ed, who lived in the house across from the rabbi, died a few years back from brain cancer too. His son now lives there with his young family, and the house abutting theirs is abandoned and falling over. It's right on the brook, along the old foundations, picturesque if you squint hard enough. Sight unseen about fifteen years ago, a family from Texas bought the place. Within days they realized their kids were imperiled by the collapsing floor and the blooms of mold climbing up the walls, but they didn't have a cent left to sue the seller. They left as quickly as they came. Maybe I made a mistake coming here, too, but at least I did my due diligence of visiting. It sits as cold comfort. And at least that little family escaped the cancer which seems to have felled their closest neighbors.

In old photographs from the gravure along the west side of the road we see "the rabbi's house," although it didn't belong to the rabbi back then. While the village is populated now with a few flatland secular Jews, somewhat typical of the Vermont demographic, what the rabbi was doing here was anyone's guess. He let his little house next to Estelle deteriorate stubbornly until it finally fetched a nice sum from a couple who used wit and skill to talk him into selling for the land.

The first and last time I ever saw the rabbi, he burst into the front door of the inn and gave me a soul kiss on the mouth. "I'm the rabbi" he crowed, sprinting out the door just as my husband rounded the corner from the breakfast room. There's something about the south end of the village. The only time I ever saw his erstwhile neighbor, the lawnmower lady, she burst in the front door as well, screaming "I'm from the village and don't ever let your dog shit on my deck again!" I followed her out onto the porch trying to explain that our dog was a rescue from an inner city, he was phobic, and never went up anyone's steps much less shit on them, but she ignored me, marching back down over the dirt and gravel shaking her fist. We'd moved in only a few days before, and it was disappointing to learn so early on that I couldn't let my kid walk alone to the post office regardless of how bucolic this place looked. Even with the white steeple of the Congregational church presiding over it all.

Coming into town from the interstate, north along the Ridge, you pass the elementary school, beige with a 1970s double-wide sensibility. It replaced the one-room schoolhouse two doors down from Estelle's and across the road from the old Parsonage just beyond our barn. The Parsonage has been a B&B for decades. Back before the dark times, as I call the days before things fell apart, way before Yom Kippur 2009, we innkeepers referred guests to one another, made quilts together, baked the occasional baklava together, and, for a period of time, I gave their cat his regular enema. The old schoolhouse, now a private home owned by the great-grand niece of the town's iconic Jessie Fisk, has a bell tower, as does The Fork Shop. I imagine the town once quite melodic as the children were called to class and the laborers were called back from lunch, the weekend slack taken up by the church just an eighth of a mile from the bridge. At one time our little village even felt to us the way it must have looked to others, the inn guests, the folks who came into town to eat at my old friend's restaurant, city people who came searching for a second home with a Rockwell vibe.

Just before Yom Kippur in 2009, a cyclone whipped down the steep six acres behind the inn from the old horse paddock and took down a three-foot-wide locust tree. I had just pulled out our drive to the road, the tree missing me by moments. I hadn't even noticed the cyclone until my husband called me on my cell phone, his usually calm demeanor shattered. Another tree, on the property line, also snapped. In the morning, we discovered that the property line marker seemingly moved a foot to the south. "Ha," my husband said. "I knew it." The neighbors came over, admitting it was their tree despite the possible marker move, and offered a portion of the clean-up costs: ten percent for their skinny punky tree. My husband told them to take the wood and use it in their fireplace, as we would be using ours. My husband clearly did not say, "Come over in your truck and take everything." A woman from up the Ridge had chainsawed the damage into movable pieces, carting off the brush and charging us $3,000. We'd been in financial crisis since moving to Vermont days before September 11th, and another three grand seemed just about right. On the Day of Atonement no less.

Sure, there are other versions of what happened next, but I was right there the whole time. Just before we needed to leave for synagogue, our neighbor backed his pickup up to the pile of good wood and filled the bed. I ran out half-dressed and told him that wasn't his wood, the stuff over there was his wood. He pretended not to hear me. He drove off, returned to take more. I picked up the nearest log and shook it at him. "I paid for it and I'm taking it," he yelled, but drove off again. My daughter hovered on the stone steps, no idea who I was at that point. Her mother was threatening a neighbor with a log? His wife rounded the then still healthy pines, all memories of baklava and shared cat enemas subsumed by rage. Seeing the log I held over my head, she retreated. I followed her until my daughter screeched from the steps.

Standing guard over my felled trees like a Hatfield or McCoy, late to synagogue, I kicked the punky logs over onto the neighbor's property where they continue to disintegrate to this day. Another word never passed between our households, but I think of them as I toss my lint.

The foundry, the gravure, and the blacksmith have long since tumbled into the brook leaving just the rickety railing of the pitchfork factory, now an Airbnb, over which I stand today, as the little pond-lake rushes under the deck and under the main road, past the post office and through the fields along Massacre Hill and becomes the brook for which the town is named.

The midline going east to west is the wooden pontoon bridge that floats over Sunset Lake. If you were to cross it from the west and not stop, you'd come right up our driveway through the remaining locust trees to Jessie Fisk's old horse barn. We have a timeworn painting of the roundabout that used to be at the foot of the driveway, and the general store with a gas pump now a town park where a granite sculpture of a hippo dad and baby sits. The only time that the hippo made sense sitting in that park was when Hurricane Irene flooded the village in 2011 and it was half underwater. But it's famous now, and the little square of green edged on the west side by Sunset Lake and the north side by an old red barn is one of the most highly photographed postcard scenes in all of central Vermont. Sometimes I see paintings of the bridge and the hippos looking up towards our barn when I'm traveling. It's like a crazy deja-vu when I'm in some Arizona gallery and I experience one of those moments when you aren't really sure where you are or where you want to be.

Usually I'm here, watching the main drag for people who let their dogs crap in the park, some days yelling across the road for them to clean it up. Some nights I'm outside yelling at the hooligans with their 4 a.m. flash mobs on the bridge. Headlights flashing, sound systems blaring, thrashing in the deep lake water. I could call the constable or the sheriff but by the time they arrive, the mob has moved on. I could say the same for calling 911. Famous as the bridge is in these parts, the young, new dispatchers have made some serious mistakes getting to it. I spent an hour once trying to revive an old man who drowned while the ambulance never came and the volunteer fire truck didn't have a defibrillator. For years I could still feel the snap of his sternum like a tiny twig under rubber.

A general store and a gas pump like in the old days would be better in my opinion, since nowadays it's a half hour drive just to get cream for your coffee and I've driven over hill and dale on gas fumes more often grateful to gravity than I'd like to admit. Decades ago, neighbors on the north side—the ritzy side as some might say, the side with the renovated old town hall and the oldest continuously running library in the state, maybe the country—decided that the intersection would be better without that roundabout. Now we have a stop sign from the north that no one pays attention to and at least a hundred times a summer my husband says how much revenue a traffic camera could generate. This is especially true when our dog runs in front of the huge manure trucks that cart the thousands of gallons of nitrogen laden waste from the once-family-farm-now-industrial-behemoth at the bottom of Massacre Hill up just over our town line into Williamstown, which may be accepting it as some sort of quid-pro-quo quietly negotiated at a town meeting once upon a time. I don't know that for a fact, but it feels right. Those trucks stop for nothing. When the gas station was dismantled, the gasoline storage tanks were illegally deposited back up on the acreage that was supposed to be ours, near the right-of-way now draped in Laurence's mother's ornamental bamboo. Which is how life works.

Jessie's barn is a landmark to the east on the edge of our property. On the south side of the barn is that damn right-of-way and to the other side is the old cape, built in 1792. The Haggett House, which, although we live in it, will never be known as the Gaby-Smith House. Even if we die in it, the other ghosts will compete for top billing and, as usual, they will win.

Poisoning isn't new to the village, as I found out a year before our relocation to the village from upstate New York. During our second or third visit I was researching the inn, the village, the quality of the lake water, the elementary school, and falling in love with what I wanted to see. I was anxious to have a midlife breakdown that did not include infidelity or a red sports car. Instead I bought a used red Subaru and a tired old inn on a six-mile dirt road.

I was alone one night in the common room of the Peck House, the larger of the inn buildings, imagining what I would do to this central room—*get rid of the dull walls and the brown sectionals, the ugly lamps and cheap framed prints*. I imagined cabbage rose overstuffed chairs, some toile on a fainting couch, and welcoming subtle pink walls in the dining area. I had looked upon past owners of the inn as simple and boringly middle class, all of them terrible decorators. It was all anything but simple, as we found out later from our lawyer who investigated the right-of-way and the ten acres which suddenly belonged to Estelle, Roland, and now the Japanese knotweed.

Distracted by color schemes, I envisioned a whole new era for the inn under my ownership, a gem on the old main road. I imagined myself no longer a healthcare worker, able to be home when my daughter got off the school bus, watching from the dining room window instead of in an office worrying every day if she got to "latchkey" alright. Latchkey, as they called it, was an after-school program run by the YMCA in our hometown. One day a well-meaning childcare worker showed the eight-year-olds his infected nipple rings, and while my daughter found it educational, I saw it as another sign to switch the landscape.

That night, I immersed myself in the town's history. I had already fallen in love with stories of Jessie Fisk and her companion Miss Butters, their presence still felt sharply throughout the inn and the village. I had begun to hear the tales of long ago—ghosts in high collars and baggy coveralls. And stories of more recent times—the deep fissures of anger along with hilarious accounts of partner-swapping back in the 1960s (or was it the 70s), the rural dirt road version of key parties. (Winters are long in Vermont; they can go on for half the year it seems. In a time before Netflix and internet porn, I guess the neighbors looked pretty good as an alternative to the utter boredom that sets in on a six mile dirt road in mid-March.)

Curled up on the brown sectional, reflections of the fire bouncing on the darkened windows as quaint snowbanks edged the road—smitten—I flipped through *The History of Brookfield, Vermont*. A more detailed account of a town's history you are not likely to find. Compiled by the Brookfield Historical Society, it was full of begettings going back to 1762, anecdotes written by townspeople long gone, family histories, tender accounts of a life that bore no relationship to my own Russian Jewish immigrant background.

Poems, ballads, grainy photographs became as fascinating as my own ancestors—"Aunt Lizzie's Coffin" among my favorites.

I was searching for anything related to the Peck House, the Haggett House, Jessie Fisk, Green Trails Inn, or the Floating Bridge. Under Peak/e, listed just before Peck, I found the story of Mrs. Rebecca Peake (nee Cummins in some reports) and I decided I was right there in her old living room, although there's no way to know if they meant the Peake home or the Peck House. On more careful scrutiny years later, the Peakes, of which there are no more in this town, clearly lived high up on East Hill, a more remote location and understandably leaving one more prone to quiet mayhem.

Rebecca, considered to be of unsound mind with a history of headaches, was charged and convicted in 1835 with the arsenic poisoning of her stepson Ephraim Peake. Despite her plea of insanity, the jury decided on hanging after only one hour of deliberation. She died quite on her own before the hanging date, February of 1836, in the Chelsea jail just aways over a picturesque set of mountains and valleys. From throat ulcers. Which makes me wonder if our insane Rebecca, who had "not so strong a mind as some" was bright enough to have secreted some arsenic into jail, determined to live and die on her own terms. Well over a century and a half before *#metoo*, one might also wonder why she poisoned Ephraim in the first place.

Intrigue. Pristine lake. A room stenciled around 1830, restored by Jessie Fisk a century later. A famous floating bridge. The ghost of Jessie, spending her days in jodhpurs and fedora, the previous owner of the Green Trails and a legend whose coattails I wanted to ride, was still leaving cigarette butts where only I could find them.

The inn had been a landmark along the dirt road. A carriage stop, famous for the hand-stenciled parlor, one of the last in the state to survive. Sustained over time as a riding school for young ladies, a restaurant, and most recently its thirteen tired rooms rented to leaf peepers, bicycling groups, quilters, and cross country skiers who roamed the back trails once groomed by Roland and his mattress frame. Neither my husband nor I had ever ridden a snowmobile, but as we had rationalized so much in this endeavor, how hard could it be?

"Let's do it," and my husband agreed.

The last time the schoolchildren visited our 1830 stenciled parlor was on the first September 11th, the day the towers fell and the teachers at our tiny school wanted the afternoon to seem as normal as possible, maybe for the last time.

The stenciling is faded, cracked, discolored, hidden for over a century until Jessie discovered it under sheets of wallpaper which she painstakingly removed to reveal the basket and flower motif. Today as I sit writing, it is another September 11th almost two decades later, and the Haggett House is our home. The owners of the restaurant on the lake, once but no longer friends, abandoned their business. The bank can't sell it. Laurence's brother will soon move south to die. The house on cinder blocks will stand cold and empty, and it's not likely his son will ever return to Vermont. The Fork Shop is all but abandoned, one family renovating and then disappearing, Miss Bette getting it for a breeze in foreclosure, but now she is pretty much gone as well. We are cozy up in the Haggett House, although Jessie's barn is losing part of its roof and we can't afford to repair it. Both the neighbors to the south, I hear, are ill. I can see lights on late into the night now that the line of pines between us is dead. I still think about sending a card.

To the north, the renovated houses on the lake now serve as second homes and there are some days in the summer when the dirt road seems congested and the sounds of children screaming in the cold lake echo days gone by. Some winters, the lake is cleared a bit and children still skate in frenzied circles, their bright hats weaving joyous patterns against the white. The ghosts quiet at those times, comforted. As am I.

The year we sold the Peck House to Miss Bette, a storm took down the chimney of that great fireplace. In typical small town synchronicity, a coworker's (I had returned to working in healthcare) father-in-law had built the fireplace and was still around, would have been happy to repair it. But

Miss Bette said her funds were limited and, by the time it came up again, the stonemason had died. The chimney remained strewn along the road for years and I had to look away whenever I passed.

HOW TO PAINT: TIPS FROM A SMALL-TOWN CONTRACTOR

KRISTINE KOPPERUD

First, you'll need to choose a color. Consider that any paint's faint undertones will come out on the wall. A greenish gray will feel green. A salmony terra cotta will read pink. You'll need two gallons for every 400 square feet. Three, if you're changing the room from a light buttercream, say, to crimson, or vice versa. Don't rely on the Glidden website, which says a single gallon goes 400 square feet. Paint-and-primer-in-one, which is standard these days, is thick. It covers better than the old latex, way better than oil-base, but it doesn't go as far.

♦

My dad grew up milking Holstein cows by hand and tuning the radio to WCCO to hear the Minnesota Twins play, lying with his fingers laced behind his head, next to his older brother, Russ, listening in the dark. Their second-story bedroom window opened to the east—the farmhouse at least 100 years old by that point—and its sheer curtain would billow in a summer breeze, the crickets singing and the damp cool seeping in by the ninth inning.

Before either of them was born, their room was the kitchen of a tiny 3-room apartment where their young aunts had lived, in succession, while their newlywed husbands were away at war. The steep stairs of the apartment emptied directly into the farmhouse kitchen, which was also crowded by the front door, a wide walnut dining table, and the washing machine in the corner. Later, my grandparents bought a small upright freezer and stood it, too, in this kitchen. We could sit around the table for holiday meals, as our numbers grew, but if one person got up to get more butter for the sweet corn or lefse, say, the people on either side also needed to stand and help free the chairs from their tight formation, scooted close under the table.

My dad graduated high school and moved away from that farm, but he spent my childhood trying to get back to it. My family visited twice or more a month, and my brother and I spent whole summers there. I came to realize that my home in Nebraska was actually my parents' starter home, in line with the teaching job I don't think my dad had intended to keep, not for 42 years, anyway. Always, they talked of moving back north, closer to "the cousins" and the still waters of lake country—of making do until the time was mysteriously right.

To make ends meet, my dad did what he'd done to put himself through college: He painted houses. Interior, exterior, new construction, remodels, barns, outbuildings, apartments turning over tenants. In 40 years in my one-stoplight hometown, well-liked by his customers, my dad painted several homes several times, with my brother and me as his crew. In addition to actual painting, I learned to drive a stick, wrenching his red Chevy S-10 paint truck through its gears, and I got handy with caulk for damaged siding and the glaze that resets loose window panes—tools that suited my dad's personal austerity just fine. He wore thrift-store running shoes to stand on ladders, both shellacked with layers of paint. When the soles of his Reeboks wore out, he swaddled them in duct tape—though his shoe-shopping itself bordered on compulsion. "Some guy died, and I got his shoes," Dad would say, wiggling the toe of his latest find in my direction, his Norwegian blue eyes twinkling. "He paid the big bucks. Me? $2.50."

But Dad's conviction ran deeper than sticker shock. As I grew old enough to understand the wages that work brings, I realized my dad always bid his paint jobs too low—not to undercut competitors, but more on principle, to exchange a kind of small-town currency meted out in hand-me-down gymnastics uniforms for me, say, or elaborate afternoon tea spreads in Mrs. Ewing's shady side yard, the condensation on our smiling Kool-Aid cups pooling onto the plastic of red-checkered tablecloth. Money, he felt, it seemed, should not come too easily, and enough really is plenty. But put another way, another day: If you undersell yourself, there are others who will, too.

◆

Remember that paint dries darker than it appears wet, so don't panic when you open the first can and it doesn't look like the color you picked, not at all. Trust the thumb smudge of it on the label on the lid, made by the woman who squirted the dark and mysterious threads of tint into the can of base, then pounded the lid back on with a rubber mallet and slung it in the agitator at the hardware store.

◆

Dad listened to radio programming like a man raising a clandestine antenna from a bunker. He was always within earshot of his prized radio, one that picked up stations around the world, and on which my brother and I weren't allowed to touch more than the power button. Dad literally whistled while he worked, too, as his father did before him. I learned "Hail to the Chief" this way, years before I knew the name for the tune or when it was traditionally played. In the catalog of my repertoire, it comes after you button on a long-sleeve shirt, for sun protection and to deflect the mist of splattering paint, and before the clattering closed of a wood-framed screen door, the kind without a hydraulic tensioner. For my dad, it came after he left NRA country for Kennedy and Luther King, Jr., and it came before his day job, teaching music. As years rolled by, teaching sounded less and less like big, brassy fanfares and more like a fugue of its own politics, with the school arts programs beaten back in favor of school sports teams, or cut down to feed the frenzy over math and science.

◆

Start by unscrewing all the outlet and light-switch plates from the walls. Set them upside down, like turtle shells, in a windowsill out of the way. Rest the screw for each in its shell. Then, stretch painter's tape along all the horizontal edges: baseboards, windows, mirrors, built-in shelves. "Painter's tape" looks like masking tape but has less aggressive adhesive that doesn't pull the paint or varnish off surfaces when removed.

To apply this tape, pull out a stretch half your wingspan. Stick the free end to the baseboard, say, aligning its edge exactly at a right angle with the wall. Reach the roll end of the tape as far as you can along the baseboard and tack it with your thumb, also at a neat right angle. Then run the flat edge of your putty knife the length of the tape, pressing it down. Then, while holding the point where you stopped, without ripping the tape from the roll, unspool another stretch and continue. This requires finesse but is faster than ripping off and applying the tape piece by piece.

Also, the right angle is critical. If you let the tape lap up on the wall in spots, you will find blotches of the original wall color beneath when you pull the tape off. You will try to cover these with a stroke from a trim brush, but you will slop some on the baseboard and have to wait for it to dry a bit to wipe it with a rag without smearing paint further. It's just better to get good with the tape-and-putty-knife technique.

◆

Dad had ideas about the kinds of work that were honorable, criteria he would wax on about in the 90 percent humidity of Midwestern July, when we would move our ladders and the paint sprayer to stay ahead of the sun, beating against a suburban split-level. Doctors, he thought, had a little too easy a time, raking in the dough for so little actual output. But rather than encourage me to game their system, as I wrote essay after essay to get myself into college on scholarship, he lobbied for careers that held some seed of the creative—and good benefits.

"You should audition for the Navy band," he announced, when he heard about an opening in the clarinet section, the instrument I played to modest acclaim. "Those guys retire early with full pension." When I pointed out the obvious risk of serving in armed conflict—reminding him that he himself had planned down to the border town how he would defect to Canada to avoid the Vietnam draft—he said only and with a laugh, "Don't worry—they don't shoot musicians." He also thought I might follow him into teaching—but only at the college level, he was clear, where I might be eligible for sabbaticals and teach just two, three classes a week. *That* kind of doctor he could be proud of.

But as the suggestions piled up, I found I couldn't crack his code: Work hard? Check. Finish what you start? Okay. Stand your ground for respect, time off, healthcare, overtime? I'm not sure when I stopped listening. I just knew that whatever he was saying wasn't what he himself was doing. He taught school nine months of the year, beleaguered by conflict with his principal and with snare-pounding, spit-valve-emptying, gossip-mongering junior-high shitheads, and he painted everything from barns to bathrooms full-time in the summers, always an underdog. Underpaid, by his own devising. Undervalued, and holding tight, it seemed, to some distant redemption he could justify if only he suffered long enough. "The three biggest reasons to become a teacher?" his favorite joke began, one he could tell without messing up the punchline. "June, July, and August."

In the meantime, I dropped out of the English education track and picked up journalism instead. I graduated summa cum laude, like he did, but instead of getting a job, I bought a bike—an expensive Gary Fisher mountain bike—and announced my plan to ride the newly mapped Great Divide Mountain Bike Route with my then-boyfriend, a tall and mouthy doctor's son. That ride turned up a job with a magazine publisher in Idaho, and I made plans to marry my companion with the fuck-you attitude. At that time, I liked his bravado. I hadn't thought ahead to when the ways in which I was still my father's daughter might put me at odds with his ambitions.

◆

If you'll be painting the ceiling, do it first. Your roller will splatter on the walls and floor while you work across the ceiling, so be sure to have drop clothes throughout. Roll on the paint in the "w" shape they teach in the Home Depot commercial, feathering the excess off the end of the roller with short, soft strokes to avoid rigid streaks and drips. Check for and smooth out drips as you go. There will be drips.

The real secret here isn't the sopping 12- or 14-inch roller with a long handle but the 4- to 6-inch hand-held roller with a felt-covered end. This recent invention allows you to roll paint into corners where walls meet and press within an inch of the ceiling and other paint-prohibitive fixtures, eliminating time-consuming follow-up with a trim brush and can of paint. Dad loved the small rollers so much he would sometimes do a whole room with the 6-inch sort, claiming that the time spent within arm's length of the wall made it easier to spot and cover areas where the paint rolled on too thinly.

Stop and move your ladder, Dad would say. Don't overreach. You'll just hit the [ceiling, window trim, cabinet, etc]. Also, stop and get more paint on your roller. Don't stretch it too thin. A too-dry roller will actually pull paint back off the wall, leaving a mottled mess that may need a full second coat.

◆

While we lived in Idaho, my young husband and I settled into what would become our pattern: I would work long hours at a job I loved for lesser but steady pay. He would pursue seasonal jobs, including professional farrier work, that amounted to as much money in a matter of months, then, as he got better, just weeks.

In his increasing free time, my husband honed expensive hobbies: upland game hunting requiring trained, purebred dogs and a lot of high-caliber gear and guns. Backcountry horsemanship, leading to horse ownership. Big powder winter sports best enjoyed with bigger boards, better goggles. Soon I felt I was playing catch-up to the enjoyment of my own life, wondering what my partner would invest in next, usually outside my knowledge and with a play-now-pay-later modus operandi. Why wasn't it mine? And if his pursuits didn't satisfy me—though often he wanted me to enjoy them, too—what *did* I want for myself?

◆

Trim speed is what separates a good painter from an amateur. It's the most finicky step, where you climb a ladder to paint that narrow margin above the reach of the roller, up to the right angle with the ceiling. If you do this right, you will not splotch the wall color on the ceiling (which is usually white), and you will apply enough paint that you may not need to go over all the trim with a second coat. But this skill takes practice.

You must learn to identify a good trim brush, for starters, with its thousands of straight, fine bristles tapering to a clean edge. This brush should be the width of your palm to carry optimum paint and leverage the full dexterity of your hand and wrist to press those bristles to a singular slant. Do not buy the wimpy brushes the width of two fingers together labeled "trim" in hardware stores. Spend the extra $16.99 on the former. If you take care of it, you might come to love this brush as much and for as long as a favorite pair of jeans.

Also a good painter is ambidextrous, able to paint trim in each direction, usually pressing the paint away from center, reaching into far corners and around light fixtures and toilets. The hand not running the paint brush will be holding the can of paint, and here it should be said that it's rarely recommendable to climb a ladder with a full can. One-third of a can will do. You can discourage paint from drizzling down the sides of the can by taking the corner of your putty knife and, when the can is new, perforating the inner rim of the can every few inches so paint that collects as you wipe excess from your brush will drain back in.

◆

My husband and I moved to Iowa, to a farm. We built a grass-fed beef company when "local food" was still a new idea. But success in the meat industry, I suspected, required more complicity with the status quo than championing anything different. I heard rumors of back rooms. Of how, once an animal's guts come out, it can be tough to tell whether it ate grass or grain. My husband, I learned, could stomach these sale-barn sleights of hand. Unsure how I was being co-opted, I painted farmers' market trailers, painted signage for grocery stores, painted pictures with words I wanted to believe were true.

My dad left teaching unceremoniously, without acknowledgment by his administrators, though generations of students continued to thank him. The school system's "age plus experience" early retirement policy paved the way to a comfortable pension, easing the chronic headaches, stiff neck, and sour stomach he put up with out of farm-bred forbearance. Together we painted every room in my house (twice), painted picnic tables for farm parties, painted a neat, wordless understanding around my husband to contain his short temper and disdain for my risk-adversity, my dogged allegiance to integrity.

Then, two years into retirement, my dad got sick. A child of the Midwestern Lymphoma Belt, handler of lead paint, asbestos, mold, mouse turds, paint thinner, construction adhesives, pesticides, herbicides, auto oil he changed himself—he was laced through with cancer. It rooted in his stomach, where it could not be excised, a stubborn patina of red across his scans.

While he was in last-ditch treatment after treatment, I lied to him about my marriage. I could hardly admit my husband had grown sick of my reservation—the kind I had inherited—and had moved on to a girl who admired his love of risk, his Midas touch amid high stakes.

Sooner than I could grasp, the time came to forgive both my dad and myself for our willingness to whitewash, to brush aside, to cover with earnest work, that which should be stripped to bare wood and examined.

◆

"The common practice of being miserable in a job creates a dangerous atmosphere which can affect growing children who see the adults they love relating negatively to their work, coming home frustrated and unhappy," wrote William Coperthwaite, author of *A Handmade Life: In Search of Simplicity*. Riveted, I copied this longhand a decade ago, late in the night, from the book I was reading. Later I typed it into notes on my laptop. Still years later, I copied it to Google Drive, where I keep the cloud archive of my life. Now I'm typing it here, keystroke by stroke:

"Imagine being able to face your kids honestly and having them know you cannot be bought—that you are among those who do not have a price. It is so much healthier for a child to see parents recognizing that their way of living is wrong and seeking a remedy rather than continuing to rationalize unhappiness, thereby encouraging the child to follow the same pattern."

◆

"Are you afraid?" I asked my dad, where we lay side by side in his hospice bed, gazing at the ceiling.

He snorted.

"I'm not sure," I think he said.

I do remember: "You're strong, 'Steen-y,"and, his standard riff on my writing: "Don't be so serious. Your funny stuff is better."

I would be the one, just hours later, to coax his eyelids shut, holding them with the pads of my thumbs, until they stayed closed, his sandy blond lashes bristling together.

◆

The color I've picked isn't quite going to cover what came before, but I will press my brush to its edge, where wall meets ceiling, pushing the trembling lip of paint ahead of it, until the line I'm making—in fact, all the legal lines I'm drawing, in a life of my own—are clean. Don't stop, Dad would say. Guide the paint until your brush goes a little dry, then wipe the remainder down the wall, dip the bristles, and start again where the line started to waver.

When I climb down the ladder and back away—the test of how true your trim is—this border will be crisp and unbroken, as good as any I could pay for. "Thanks," I will say to myself, to him. It's not everything, but it's real.

"Life skill! This is a *life* skill, Steen-y," Dad fondly (and frequently) joked, when my teenage self had eyes only for quitting time—maybe cruising Main Street in my friend's mauve Buick LeSabre—and he push-pulled me, sweat-sour, to a more rewarding end to the day. The breeze would finally sneak in cool around us, where we squatted in grass damp with evening, passing a gushing garden hose between us. This was ritual, the cleaning of brushes, working loose eight or more hours of sludgy color with the flat of our putty knives and slapping the wet bristles against our thighs to see how much milky paint still emerged from their depths. Then we would fold each brush into its original card cover, the kind with a wrap-around tie fastener, this house's palette mingling with some of the homes before it, and the one before that, and before that, a record of where we've been. It's a hard living but honest, its ratio of effort to fulfillment fixed.

Mrs. Ewing and her tea tarts are gone. Dad is gone. Even our house in that small Nebraskan town, where our ladders and scaffolding laid like lawn art in the yard, is gone, sold off its foundation, the lot now overgrown by trees.

But I am here, pushing forward, from my solid center, toward edges I can't yet see but that I'm equipped to meet, and handily.

LAST STAND IN THE CLOSING COUNTRY

CHRISTOPHER COCCA

Black Cat Bone was covering Clapton and Dylan and promised anyone a free beer for naming one of the Yardbirds. I named three on the spot—didn't get three beers, though, and damned if I wasn't thirsty. We drink Yuengling out here, out in the towns and fading country outposts that patch Pennsylvania together under aging highway ribs. Yuengling's dark and good and constant and anywhere you go they just call it lager and everyone knows what you mean.

Out in the beer garden the band introduced "Watchtower" by telling us it was a Dylan song everyone thinks Hendrix wrote and I wondered if they were serious. The solos were tight, though, I had to give them that. Three lead guitars, a bass and a set of drums. Sweet Les Paul fuzz dripped off the youngest one, and he traded blues duties with a middle aged man playing clean Fender licks, woo-ee-oo, just like Buddy Holly, Buddy Holly young and sweaty, Buddy Holly the godfather of punk. Paternity test pending.

This was Black Cat's last stand, one final gig for the Berks County faithful gathered at the Kutztown Fair. Across the midway local kids line danced to some new Nashville schlock and on the other end of the fairgrounds the rides went dark and I walked to the parking lot thinking about Southern rock and Johnny Cash and paradox. The sweet guitar fuzz, the slick syncopation, the trucker hats and shiny belt buckles worn by people who weren't trying to be ironic. I imagined the spot on NPR, some whitebread cat in wire rims talking about all of this as sort of symbol, some kind of microcosm of rural Americana, these summer rituals, these country fairs and carnivals and gigs. I heard them laugh and I heard the canned sound bites, the clinking grill tools and bleating sheep. Symbols and sound bites and ten summers gone and no one out here listens to NPR anyway.

This place is in me, though, and it runs pretty deep. The family business is concessions and we're out here all the time. The land is disappearing, plowed under by suburbs and the higher costs of living in New Jersey and New York and America's new colonists reap concrete and sprawl. The line dancers act like they don't see it coming—they've got their steps down and it's something to see. The blues singers, well the blues singers are just passing through, aren't they? They're a soundtrack, a soundtrack on its last cut giving back beat to the crises you bring in with you and you think you hear redemption when they solo. Tonight, though, tonight it's just crisis. Tonight it's bulldozers and by-passes and subdivisions, tonight it's the change I know is coming. Knowing this will all end soon, that these parts will finally fall and these people with them, paved under one of a million concrete slabs connecting New York and Philly and Baltimore, too, like an old song everyone thinks someone else wrote, and I find myself wondering if I'm serious.

ABOUT THE CONTRIBUTORS

Joan Taylor Cehn is a retired clinical speech pathologist. A graduate of Northwestern University, she practiced for many decades in hospitals throughout the San Francisco Bay Area. In 2008 she co-edited and contributed to the anthology *Writin' On Empty: Parents Reveal The Upside, Downside, And Everything In Between When Children Leave The Nest.* She currently lives in a small seaside town on the central coast of California where she pursues fun and adventure. She cherishes and is grateful for her loving family and many life-long friends throughout the country.

Chris Cocca is from Allentown, Pennsylvania. His work has been published at venues including *Hobart, Brevity, Pindeldyboz, elimae, The Huffington Post, O:JAL, Rejection Letters, Mineral Lit Mag, Schuylkill Valley Journal, Perhappened, Anti-Heroin Chic, Feed, Appalachian Review, Bandit Fiction, Still, VIA Voices in Italian Americana, Belt, The Shore*, and *Dodging the Rain*. He is a recipient of the Creager Prize for Creative Writing at Ursinus College and earned his MFA in creative writing at The New School. In 2021, *The Shore* nominated his poem, "The Effects of Ground-Level Ozone on the Ecology of Pennsylvania Highways," for the Pushcart Prize.

Kimberly Ence is a recent MFA graduate from Columbia University. She's a native Idahoan. Her earliest writing was done on this thing called a typewriter and self-published on a mimeograph (go ask your grandma). You'll find her latest work in *JuxtaProse* (2018 Nonfiction Prize winner), *The Eastern Iowa Review, Utah@125, Columbia Journal*, and elsewhere. She's a mother of five, adjunct English instructor, and snow enthusiast. Kim lives in Park City, Utah, with her husband, teenage son, and Kona the Akita. For this piece, Kim had access to her father's private memoir and permission to quote, for which she is grateful.

Linda Hansell is a writer and educator based in Philadelphia, Pennsylvania. Her essays have appeared in *The Emerald Coast Review, Months to Years,* and *Wising Up Press*. In addition to writing essays, Linda helps other people write their memoirs or autobiographies and has co-authored four such books (the latest from Skinner House Books.) She is also a musician and bird lover.

Melissa Hart is an author and journalist living in Eugene, Oregon. Visit her website: www.melissahart.com.

Nina Gaby is a writer, visual artist, and psychiatric nurse practitioner who spent the pandemic hunkered down across from the longest floating bridge east of the Mississippi with her dog, two cats, husband, and the Cuomo brothers on TV. She did not finish the memoir-in-progress from which this piece was taken, did not develop any interest in sourdough or needlepoint, but has suddenly emerged with a whole new level of appreciation for the resilience of our collective spirit. Please note—some names and events in "Looking South on Main," except for those of a historic nature, have been changed or made into composite form. Visit www.ninagaby.com for a complete list of publications and images of Gaby's mixed-media artwork.

Lindsay Gelay-Akins is a teacher who lives in New Jersey with her husband, her three young children, and her dog. She has no spare time right now, but if she did you would likely find her on the beach reading novels. This is her first print publication.

Kristine Kopperud is a writer and editor in rural Northeast Iowa. Her creative nonfiction has won the Diana Woods Memorial Award for Nonfiction at Lunch Ticket and appears at *HuffPost*, Parents.com, *River Teeth, The Girlfriend* (AARP), *MUTHA Magazine, Literary Mama*, and in several anthologies. Her hermit-crab essay "Jaw Wiring: What You Need to Know" was a flash nonfiction winner at *Sweet: A Literary Confection*, appeared in *Creative Nonfiction*'s Sunday Short Reads, and was nominated for a Pushcart Prize.

Dyann Nashton is a freelance writer from Central New York. She holds a bachelor's degree in journalism from Utica College and her career carried her from the newsroom through not-for-profit public relations, marketing, and fund development. Today, she works for a charitable foundation. In her spare time, she practices and teaches yoga.

Suzanne Samuels writes creative nonfiction, children's realistic fiction, and adult historical fiction. She is fascinated by the centrality of narrative in human life and how story helps us learn about the world. Her latest novel in progress, *The Engraver*, was inspired by a 1922 tenement fire that killed most of her grandfather's family and left him maimed. In researching the fire, Suzanne discovered a great-great aunt, who was never spoken about but who likely saved her grandfather's life. *The Engraver* explores the ways family both protects and constrains us, and the sacrifices we make on behalf of others.

Kelly Garriott Waite writes from Oberlin, Ohio, where she's researching and writing about the life of the second owner of her 1908 Arts & Crafts home, a woman left out of the house's written history. Her work has appeared in *Barren Magazine, BioStories, Tributaries: the Fourth River*, and elsewhere.

Melissa Scholes Young is the author of the novels *The Hive* and *Flood*, and editor of *Grace in Darkness* and *Furious Gravity*, two anthologies by women writers. She is a contributing editor at *Fiction Writers Review*, and her work has appeared in the *Atlantic, Ms., Washington Post, Poets & Writers, Ploughshares, Literary Hub*, and *Believer Magazine*. She has been the recipient of the Bread Loaf Bakeless Camargo Foundation Residency Fellowship, the Center for Mark Twain Studies' Quarry Farm Fellowship, and the Virginia Center for Creative Arts Fellowship. Born and raised in Hannibal, Missouri, she is an associate professor in literature at American University.

ABOUT THE EDITOR

Donna Talarico is founder of the independent, volunteer-led Hippocampus Magazine and Books and its annual conference, HippoCamp.

Donna, who makes her living as an independent writer and content strategist, has more than two decades of experience in marketing and communications; about half of that time has been in higher education. She's had past lives in radio promotions and television production—and if we're going way back, newspaper salesperson, ice cream scooper, and ski resort boot technician.

Donna regularly speaks at higher education and publishing conferences, writes an adult learner enrollment marketing column for Wiley Education, and has contributed to *Currents* (a higher education trade publication), *The Guardian's* Higher Education Network, *The Writer*, *mental_floss*, *Games World of Puzzles*, the *Brevity* blog, and other mainstream and trade publications. Her creative nonfiction appears in *The Superstition Review*, *The Los Angeles Review*, *The Los Angeles Times*, and *Wanderlust Journal*.

Donna teaches/has taught about branding and digital identity in the graduate creative writing and publishing programs at Wilkes University and Rosemont College, as well as at Pennsylvania College of Art & Design. She has an MFA in creative writing from Wilkes University and an MBA from Elizabethtown College.

She lives in Lancaster, Pennsylvania, with her husband, Kevin Beerman and their cat. She loves road trips, national parks, board games, greasy-spoon diner breakfasts, and museums.

ACKNOWLEDGEMENTS

Books by Hippocampus would like to thank Marshall Warfield (director) and the graduate publishing program at Rosemont College in Pennsylvania. Students in the program's Small Press Practices course (in the fall of 2020) actively participated in the selection process for this anthology, as well as in the early editing and marketing planning phases.

One of the cool things about the Rosemont graduate program is that it's made up of students of all backgrounds and ages and stages in their careers—some coming into writing and publishing after years in another industry—so the insight and expertise they collectively brought to this project was incredibly valuable.

So, this project comes to life with sincere gratitude for:

- Lauren Bruce
- Natalie Burke
- Johan Espinal
- Grace Hohn
- Sara Kiiskila
- Rachel Kolman
- Sawyer Lovett

We'd also like to thank Carla Spataro, director of the MFA in creative writing program at Rosemont College for her support. Through the school's unique dual degree program, many of the students who helped with this publishing project were also actively and simultaneously pursuing their MFAs.

One final note about this collaboration with the Rosemont students. This was a particularly challenging semester because we were in the throes of a then-new pandemic, which presented obstacles for all of us personally, professionally, and academically. The course, which was originally planned for an on-the-ground experience, had to be adapted into an online course. Additionally, *The Way Things Were* series was put on hold, as many things were during the pandemic. So it's extra special for me to see this book finally come to life knowing that these students had a role in it, during a tumultuous time at that.

Main is the second collaboration with the graduate publishing program at Rosemont College. *Ink*, the first, was worked on a year earlier and released in tandem with *Main*.

In addition to the members of this Rosemont class, we'd also like to thank three Hippocampus Magazine interns who also read both journal and book submissions (including for *Main*) as part of their volunteer experience: Karen Bellavance-Grace from Bay Path University's MFA in creative nonfiction program, Danah Lassiter from Wilkes University's Maslow Family Graduate Program in Creative Writing, and Katherine Pettine from Rosemont College's graduate publishing program.

Thank you, also, to the designers, typesetters, and proofreaders who helped bring this book to life: Lindsay Enochs, Rachel Doughtery, and Dale Louise Mervine.

Finally, much, much gratitude for the Hippocampus Magazine and Books team for making this organization and community as strong as it is. You keep this going.

– Donna Talarico, Publisher

ALSO FROM BOOKS BY HIPPOCAMPUS

GETTING TO THE TRUTH: THE CRAFT AND PRACTICE OF CREATIVE NONFICTION

DOODLING FOR WRITERS

Rebecca Fish Ewan

DIG: A PERSONAL PREHISTORIC JOURNEY

Sam Chiarelli

BY THE FORCES OF GRAVITY: AN ILLUSTRATED MEMOIR

Rebecca Fish Ewan

THE WAY THINGS WERE THINGS WERE ANTHOLOGY SERIES:

Air

Dine

Main

SELECTED MEMORIES: FIVE YEARS OF HIPPOCAMPUS MAGAZINE